CHARLOTTE GAMBILL

BEYOND

Published in Great Britain in 2019 by Charlotte Gambill
charlottegambill.com

The moral right of the author has been asserted
A CIP record of this book is available from the British Library
ISBN: 9780956856463

BEYOND

Now to Him who is able to do immeasurably more than all we ask or imagine, according to His power that is at work within us, to Him be glory in the church and in Christ Jesus throughout all generations, for ever and ever!

Ephesians 3:20-21

The word of God is heaven's invitation to increase in our ability to imagine more, ask greater and believe beyond. What if you were to not just read these words but actually act on them? What more could you discover, encounter, attain? This book is a tour guide to some beyond adventures. Each chapter asks you to take a step further and journal your journey into the more God has for your life. This devotional invites you to gain a fresh perspective of your limitless God and ask yourself, where do I need to go beyond?

We can all remember back to the time in our life when we were much younger in age but also much smaller in size. When our childish perspective saw things through much simpler lenses. When our inquisitive nature made us question things that, as we grew older, we began to just accept. I remember as a young girl going into shops that would have countertops way higher than my eye line could reach. I would stand in front of the bland looking counter knowing that just a little further up was a whole world of possibility. One of the most frustrating places was below the countertop of our local fish and chip shop, where my parents would take me to order that traditional English takeaway. I was unable to see but the sound of the fryer sizzling and the smell of the chips cooking would reach me. I knew above the ledge limiting my view was a whole different experience. If only I could just get someone to lift me up, I would be able to see what was beyond.

That experience reminds me again and again that even though our size may no longer be an inhibitor of our vision, spiritually we can live with a shrunken posture beneath too many restrictive counters. Our inquisitive nature that once moved us to ask, beg, plead to be lifted up so we could see, settles down and becomes more polite. We adjust to the restricted view, like it's the only view. When we fail to keep the longing to see beyond, we settle into living with what we know. Yet I have a sense God wants us to keep that childlike posture as a permanent fixture in our hearts and minds. A posture that trusts that He is the God who has no limits to His grace, goodness, love and peace; that He has adventures and encounters that are designed to move us beyond. We all have to go on the journey of reacquaintance with our younger self, to have no fear to ask to be lifted up so we can see and experience beyond.

So this book is asking: where do you need to go beyond? Where have you got stuck or given up desiring to see more and know more? A heart that wants to go beyond is not about being ungrateful with what you have right now but being willing to keep journeying into the more God has for your life. Within these pages you will discover a new companion, a voice that pushes you past comfort into adventure, a voice that calls to you to come to the ledge and look over.

Remember the scene in Toy Story when Buzz is the gift Andy receives for his birthday? (If the answer is no, then you need to go beyond your movie selection and watch Toy Story today.) This is a new, exciting and full of possibilities toy. The scene plays out, the young boy pulls the cord on the toy and lights dazzle him as the words "to infinity and beyond" are uttered by Buzz. Words Andy has never heard from his small toy box before, words that are going to make a few people uncomfortable but also redefine what is possible. Buzz is a believer in beyond, even when faced with opposition. His programming tells him that there is something greater out there, there is an adventure around every corner waiting to be discovered.

I pray that this book will be the Buzz Lightyear thrown into the toy box of your soul, challenging your all too familiar Woody perspective of life. I hope when you pick it up, it shouts at you "let's go beyond in areas where we have become bound", "let's get beyond our level of understanding and beyond in our realm of asking". We serve a God who created "infinity and beyond". We all need a little more of Buzz in our lives as we examine, over the next few months, some areas to go beyond. The challenge will be set for you to do things that move you into the direction of the future you believe for. This book is asking you to try something new, let some things go, say yes or say no, reconnect with the inquisitive nature of your younger self. Maybe as part of this beyond journey you will plan a trip, make a new relationship, try a new activity, ask bigger or just be braver! So friend, let's go "to infinity and beyond" together!

Charlotte Gambill

HOW TO USE THIS BOOK

———

BEYOND

So as you get ready to go beyond, let's look at how to use this book. Each chapter is divided into three sections - three thoughts built around scriptures that teach us about going beyond in a certain area of your life. The chapter finishes with suggestions of ways you can challenge yourself and ways in which you can apply this beyond thinking to your individual situation. There are also pages left blank for you to journal the thoughts that these devotionals stir in your heart.

There is no hurry to get to the end of each chapter. I encourage you to spend time meditating on each thought. Sometimes we can rush past things that we will only find in the stillness. There are 12 chapters so you can pace it out across 12 months. Read the scripture that introduces each section and then take the time to read around it too, immerse yourself in the whole chapter of God's word. When you are ready, move on to the next section. Take stock of what you have read and then go into the challenge section. Some of these are practical, some are spiritual. Some you may feel you can complete with ease, others may involve a wrestle with yourself or even with God. Be honest with Him, record how you feel and what you are asking of Him. One day you may well return to these notes and see that your life has moved beyond many of those 'countertops' that we so often become restricted by.

See It: this section is for some personal reflection, a chance to examine your heart and challenge yourself on how you are thinking and whether this lines up with God's plans for your life. Say It: this section is a chance to articulate the actions you are going to take, either through prayer, through conversations with others or through journaling your commitment. Do It: this section is where you put your plans into action, to step out into the beyond you have discovered is awaiting you.

My prayer is that over the next 12 months, as you work through the pages prepared for you here, you will begin to believe for so much more and say yes to going beyond, even when it may be a little confusing. I pray step by step, you will see your heart opening up to more possibilities, your hands saying yes to more responsibilities and your life growing and stretching into the wide open spaces that God invites you to explore, as He takes your hand and says, daughter, let Me take you beyond.

BEYOND DEVOTIONAL JOURNAL

——————————

CONTENTS

CHAPTER ONE

BEYOND ADVENTURE

BEYOND ADVENTURE

When Jesus looked up and saw a great crowd coming toward Him, He said to Philip, "Where shall we buy bread for these people to eat?" He asked this only to test him, for He already had in mind what He was going to do. Philip answered Him, "It would take more than half a year's wages to buy enough bread for each one to have a bite!" Another of His disciples, Andrew, Simon Peter's brother, spoke up, "Here is a boy with five small barley loaves and two small fish, but how far will they go among so many?"

John 6:5-9

We all have a level of adventure we permit ourselves to embark upon. We have an invisible line in our minds we can go all the way to the edge of but never dare to cross. The line is for us where the adventure ends and we see only danger beyond that point. These lines we have created in our minds are not to prohibit but to protect, we think they are sensible. While we all need to know our limits and not place ourselves in unnecessary danger, we also need to ensure that we have not allowed fear to be the one who has the final say.

Have you ever been somewhere and seen an area that is taped off with signs that say no access beyond this point? We assume that boundary is there for good reason and so don't ask any questions. However, sometimes we do need to challenge the advice; sometimes we need to understand that the lines we can end up stuck behind are keeping you and me from an adventure that awaits beyond.

I was in an airport with people lined up all around the building waiting to get through security. I was so late for my flight and I knew I was not going to make it unless I found a quick way through. I saw, right at the far side of the airport, a passport control area with hardly anyone using it. I couldn't understand why no one was going through the checkpoint so I began to head over there and on the way I discovered the problem. Several signs were hung before that line that said no entry but I could see people going through. I went to explore and discovered those signs were for a different security point that was no longer there. All those people who were potentially going to miss their flights were standing in the long line because they had been misled by the signs. How many times can this take place spiritually; where are we assuming there are some no entry points? We actually need to ask the question, is this even true? Where has our thinking got stuck behind a line someone else has drawn or where is our faith prisoner to the invisible lines of fear? I am convinced we all have some beyond adventures waiting for us but in order to take them, we are going to have to do some soul searching and line changing.

Beyond Manageable

When we become good managers we often settle for less adventure. I am a huge advocate for order and things being done well so believe me when I say, this has been hard for me to understand and apply. Yet sometimes we are managing ourselves out of miracles that others are getting to handle because our need for two times two to make four doesn't work when God's the one doing the multiplication. After teaching the crowds, Jesus asked the disciples how they would feed the thousands gathered. The disciples tried to inform Jesus that this was not only a crazy idea, it was impossible. They began to work out the scenarios and then informed Jesus that the mathematics didn't make sense: it would cost too much, the shops weren't open. Jesus was trying to give them an adventure beyond the boundaries of their manageable strategic thinking.

It took a young boy who had a beyond mindset to make this miracle happen. His five loaves and two fish were obviously nowhere near enough provision to fix this problem but this young boy was not thinking about how the division of his food could become the provision for the crowd. He was looking at the one whose hands he was placing the lunch in. He knew Jesus had ways and means he could never conceive to answer situations so he went beyond logic and embarrassment, beyond worrying about what others would say. He believed that a miracle may well be possible if he would step beyond what was permissable. Jesus was about to take what others overlooked and make so much provision there would be baskets of bread leftover. The adventure of multiplication lies beyond the lines of management so don't be closed to the miracle of God's mathematics that often makes no sense at all.

How much of your life have you managed so well you no longer need a miracle? Where is it so in order and so controlled you have no room for something that may move you into the best form of being out of control? The greatest adventures I have experienced in my life have required me to move from managing to trusting. I have had to rub out the line that says this makes no sense and press into the God that invites me beyond.

A few years ago, I had an invitation placed in my world that was very unusual, an opportunity to go and stay with a family that I didn't even know. I was told when the dates were and where I was heading but that was all the information I was given. My need to manage what came next was going into overdrive and yet I knew if I tried to manage the situation I would most likely lose out and possibly ruin the whole experience. I did something that was so out of my comfort zone and said yes, finding myself on an adventure that would actually change my life forever.

After a few days away with this incredible family and a bunch of other people who I had never met but who had also nervously said yes, I asked my kind host why no information was given ahead of time and why so many things were left unanswered. Their reply: the ones who need all that stuff never make it this far. I remember those words, they are etched in my mind. The adventure was always extended to me but the need to manage it could steal it from me.

Where is your over analysis and over controlling drawing lines that maybe it's time to erase? What college course do you need to say yes to? Where do you need to plant that seed? Who do you need to reach out to? I am not advocating chaotic irresponsibility but I am suggesting some miracles may well need you to resign from the board of management, retire from the health and safety committee or step down from your self-appointed post of quality control, so you can say yes to some new and possibly scary assignments.

"

HE WANTS YOU TO EMBRACE ADVENTURES BECAUSE HE KNOWS YOU HAVE GREATER WITHIN YOU

BEYOND EASY

Jesus sat down opposite the place where the offerings were put and watched the crowd putting their money into the temple treasury. Many rich people threw in large amounts. But a poor widow came and put in two very small copper coins, worth only a few cents. Calling His disciples to Him, Jesus said, "Truly I tell you, this poor widow has put more into the treasury than all the others. They all gave out of their wealth; but she, out of her poverty, put in everything - all she had to live on."

Mark 12:41-44

We often like the adventures we know we will be successful in. We embrace the challenge we have enough confidence to complete. We sit the test we know we have revised for. We need to be willing to move beyond what's easy into what's a little more stretching. At school the pupils get put into sets according to ability but sometimes the set assigned to an individual is not a good match and they are placed in a class that is not a stretch for that student. This happened with our son when he first went to high school. He was in a set for his maths that he was coasting through, we actually were those parents that went to the teacher and said, make it harder for him, push him up a set, he has an ability beyond where he has been placed. He did not thank us for it at the time because now he had moved from not really having to apply himself that much to having to concentrate more and do the work. He had gone from top of the class to trying to find his place in the new set. Yet that shift for our son allowed his ability to flourish. In life we can allow ourselves to be in the wrong set, we can downgrade our ability and our courage and live in the easy, saying we are not built for an adventure beyond. What if you are missing a whole new world because you have allowed yourself to take the easy option? It may be great to get the top mark in the lower set but what if you are capable of even better marks when you have to learn more and apply yourself in a different way?

Easy is often what our need to appear 'together' demands. We don't want to seem out of our depth; we want to accomplish things and move on but easy is not our friend. It will not awaken the adventures that risk will. You can have a tidy life or an adventurous life; occasionally you can have both but God is often untidy as He is a God of destiny. He wants you to embrace adventures because He knows you have greater within you. What area of your life has become easy, where you really don't even have to try anymore? Where is your kindness stuck or your willingness hijacked by the familiar things you keep saying yes to? Where is your level of understanding cruising on easy mode? We can keep our love in bottom set and just love the ones who are easy to love or we can take the challenge and move beyond easy and choose to love even our enemies. We can give from a place that's easy like the rich who threw their offering in as Jesus watched from the sidelines or we can give like the widow who gave all she had when she placed her two coins in the offering that day. Jesus noticed this woman as she was not giving what was easy, she was giving way beyond. Her risk in letting go of everything she had, moved her life way beyond what the giving of the rich who went before her could ever attain.

CHAPTER TWO

Our lives have modes and we get to choose the mode we want to live in. Just like when you play a computer game, it gives you an option: player mode easy, intermediate or hard. You know when you select each of these levels the game will adapt to your choice: the villain you may fight on the easy level is very different from the one on the hardest level and that fact in itself may be enough reason for you to stick to easy. Yet doing life on the easy mode is rarely thrilling and it can even become predictable and boring, so perhaps you need to select a new setting.

Exercise used to be something I avoided at all costs but one day I challenged myself and I started walking, which was a huge change to my lifestyle. When I had been walking for a while someone said to me, you will start running soon. I refused to believe them and said I was not a runner, to me that was way too hard to even think about. It wasn't until about six months later that I discovered that they were right, I had become bored with walking and wanted to push myself further and so now found I had started jogging and it wasn't long until I was picking up the pace and running. Now, years later, I still find it weird when people say, so you're a runner, as in my mind that's not what I am but the truth is I do run miles every day. The very thing I said I couldn't do I love to do. The way I got there was rubbing out one invisible line after another. The line that says you can't do it, the line that says you're not fit enough, the line that says stick to something easier. Easy is an option in every area of our lives but just because it's an option doesn't mean you should choose it.

Having friendships at the easy level where we just keep things on the surface is less demanding and exhausting but nowhere near as rewarding as going beyond the trivial into building something more special. I have found giving what doesn't cost me a lot is easy but giving where I know if God doesn't show up it could really stretch me is a far greater adventure. Beyond easy needs new commitments, more consideration of what you believe and how deeply you can trust what you say you hold as truth. Going beyond easy is a risk but I believe for many of us there are huge parts of our lives that are undeveloped because we have allowed ourselves to get stuck in the wrong line or be placed in the wrong set. So where is it time to go beyond what you know you can easily do and into a new level of learning and excelling?

BEYOND
FEAR

As Jesus was walking beside the Sea of Galilee, He saw two brothers, Simon called Peter and his brother Andrew. They were casting a net into the lake, for they were fishermen. "Come, follow Me," Jesus said, "and I will send you out to fish for people." At once they left their nets and followed Him.

Matthew 4:18-20

Fear is that unwanted but always willing travelling companion. It's that voice we don't want to hear but inevitably all too often allow to speak. Fear is the red pen through so many pending adventures. That's why we need to move beyond fear. Fear begins drawing lines very early on in our journey through life, reinforcing our weaknesses and feeding our lack of confidence. It uses as many failures as possible to barricade us out of even trying something different but fear is a liar and its end goals are not to protect you but to prohibit you. That's why if you want beyond adventures then you need to move beyond fear.

A few years ago, I had to move beyond fear when I said yes to something I knew was going to be a beyond adventure for me. For years, our friends had asked us to go skiing as a family with them. My kids were keen, my husband, who loves to ski, was desperate to say yes but my fear was making my no very loud and clear. I had so many fears I would have to overcome to even begin to consider this: the fear of heights; the fear of falling; the fear of being out of control; the fear of hurting myself. My responsible mind was in overdrive and for every picture they painted of fun, outings, adventures and memories of a lifetime, my fear would reply. Eventually I realised my no was also shutting down the adventure for my kids who had no such fears and wanted to try something new. So my mum heart overrode my head and I said yes. The plan was all along to just play it safe. The first day I remember getting into the cable car and as we went higher and higher my fear got louder and louder: what was I thinking? This was going to be a disaster. The only way this fear would be broken was by me deciding to go for it. I stood at the top of the mountain so scared and aware the next choice would change everything. I could ride back down to the bottom of the mountain in the cable car or ski down. My kids just took off with no fear and not even thinking about falling. I watched how they effortlessly embraced the challenge and with that, I set off behind them (not so effortlessly). I had an instructor alongside me and my friends were all there to help and encourage me but no matter how great their efforts, only one person could silence the fear and that was me.

The whole way down the mountain I was having an inner conversation. Each time I felt out of control I had to not let fear shut me down. I eventually made it to the bottom of the mountain but I knew if I was really going to go beyond fear, I needed to go back and do it again until this fear turned into fun. So back up the mountain I went until the voice of fear became quieter and quieter. On the third time around

I had a fall and I remember my friend saying, you need to fall so you can see you can get back up and she was right. Now the fear of falling had lost its power too and the very things fear told me would stop me were actually becoming the things that were helping me.

Fear wants to keep you off the mountain. It wants you to take the cable car back down. It wants you to imagine the fall will be so bad it's not worth even trying but fear is a liar. Your best life will at times require you to do what freaks you out so faith can remove the lines that fear has erected. On my physical mountain, I had to put faith in myself. I had to put faith in the instruction I had been given and faith in the fact that the fall might happen but I would get back up.

Where do you need to say yes to a new mountain? Where do you need to have an argument with fear until you settle the dispute that is currently denying access to the adventure? Fear could have kept the disciples from following Jesus; fear could have prevented Peter from stepping out of the boat; fear could have kept Paul in prison and Gideon in a wine press. Fear could have stolen Esther's voice and robbed David of his future. Fear draws lines all day everyday; they are erratic and chaotic. They are many and they criss cross every part of the path, trying to block you from writing any new chapters. Perhaps for you it's not a physical activity like it was for me, it's the fear to love, the fear to speak up, the fear to challenge. Whatever the fear, there is an adventure beyond it but it will require some new skills to be learnt, some new confessions to be spoken and maybe even some new company to keep, who instead of talking you off the mountain, will cheer you on all the way down.

BEYOND
ADVENTURE

THE CHALLENGE

SEE IT

This month I challenge you to embrace a new mountain. The first way in which you can begin to do that is by starting to see the mountain top you want to climb and identifying the place where you know you have got stuck behind some invisible lines. Where are the areas you are in easy mode, perhaps in your giving, work life or relational world? Where is the level you are living at blocking you from seeing a new adventure that awaits beyond? Where has the fear of not succeeding stopped you from trying or the fear of rejection stopped you asking or applying? Take time to see new possibilities, journal and start to incubate a vision that will broaden your horizon.

SAY IT

Now it's time for you to start articulating that vision, write down some mountains you want to begin to climb. It might be something physically in your life or you might be behind some lines spiritually. You may need to go beyond in your trust and knowledge of God. Start to plan your ascent: there will be steps you need to take at base camp before you begin to climb, so map out in words or even draw the mountain. Then begin to examine areas where your current conversations and confessions need to align with your plan. It may seem a small thing but your words have power and being deliberate in the things you say in this area will give you the confidence to actually do what it takes.

DO IT

Plan out this month activities that are taking you closer to your beyond adventure. Find people who can help advise you and encourage you. How can you equip yourself before you start? If your challenge is physical, then begin by finding out what you need to embrace this new adventure, what changes you need to make: sign up for a class, buy the running shoes. If your challenge is spiritual, where can you take a leap of faith? Maybe for you it's pressing into God at a new level, perhaps fasting for the first time or making a regular, dedicated time to pray. It could be volunteering to serve in a new area or beginning to trust God for your finances in a new way.

Start to activate each step and record your process. When fear shows up, journal how it sounds and what triggers that voice. By acknowledging the fear, you can address it until you have the confidence to rule out the lines it draws. Make a list of the things that try to prohibit you and then begin a list of things you will do to get past these obstacles. Embrace your new adventure and believe you can conquer your mountain.

NOTES

CHAPTER TWO

BEYOND
LOVE

BEYOND LOVE

If I speak in the tongues of men or of angels, but do not have love, I am only a resounding gong or a clanging cymbal. If I have the gift of prophecy and can fathom all mysteries and all knowledge, and if I have a faith that can move mountains, but do not have love, I am nothing. If I give all I possess to the poor and give over my body to hardship that I may boast, but do not have love, I gain nothing. Love is patient.

1 Corinthians 13:1-4

I remember the first time I saw a heart up close, it was in my school biology lesson and I am pretty sure I passed out. It certainly didn't look like the pretty red heart icon I had grown up seeing; this purplish small muscle looked anything but the symbol of romance, in fact it resembled something from a horror movie. However, the heart's capacity to rhythmically pump blood through our bodies and keep oxygen flowing means this small organ goes way beyond what it looks capable of. From the outside, it doesn't make much of an impression but when it is attached to the rest of the body, its potential and immense capability is evident.

When it comes to how God made you and me, He has mirrored in the spiritual so many things from the natural. Our heart spiritually is also full of possibility and its best function is when we attach it to the great commission that God has invited us all to be a part of. It has potential that goes way beyond comprehension and logic. It is designed to love beyond borders and in a way that removes boundaries. It is made to expand and grow continually and is only restricted from doing so by our openness to embrace the very things that will ask it to increase. Our heart's capacity is linked to our willingness, it is when we say yes to stretching and increasing the way we express our love that we begin to see just how powerful the spiritual muscle of our heart is.

In 1 Corinthians 13 we are told of the type of love that goes beyond. This love is a challenge to us all and gives every heart some homework to do. Often our love can become limited or liberated by what we have experienced, the good and the bad of life becomes a filter through which we love. If we are loved well, we tend to be more open to loving widely. In the places where we feel we have been hurt and mistreated, the first casualty is always our heart. If we are not careful, we can respond by shrinking back; love can become based on others' actions rather than our own values. We can train our hearts to give reciprocal responses; if you love me, I will love you. However, our model is not what others do to us but what God did for us. God is love and that changes everything: the very definition of love is now no longer found in others' behaviour but is instead defined by our Creator.

So how do we begin to take our love to the next level? How do we move our love from neutral to overdrive? Where can we lift the love we are currently expressing to a love that is exceeding? Think about where in your own life love has left its mark. Where did someone's kindness, generosity, patience, exceed all expectations?

CHAPTER TWO

Those moments we remember because they are not the typical way we see, hear or feel love.

I remember this happening when I was first introduced to my friend, Bob Goff. It was a God orchestrated meeting in America a few years ago and we ended up having a long conversation in the middle of a hotel lobby. I was so impacted by the way Bob took the time to show interest and such kind concern for me and my family when we had only just met. The love my dear friend Bob was expressing was something that would go on to mark the life of myself and my family forever. If you have ever read his book, Love Does, you will understand a little more of the impact love can have. I began to realise as I sat in the presence of this expressive and assertive love that my own heart needed to flex some more muscle. We all need those people in our world that encourage us to move beyond, to view our heart not as ordinary but as extraordinary.

Love is powerful. It has its own vocabulary, it speaks a beautiful language. It is a thoughtful and fierce companion on this journey through life. It is all the things that Corinthians teaches us. So why don't we dive into this challenge to take our love beyond by asking ourselves honestly, where has my love become lazy and where is it in need of a cardio workout? I guarantee that the journey of loving beyond won't be easy and will ask things of you that may make you feel uncomfortable. However, when we say yes to deepening our willingness to live out love, we start to see and hear things we previously passed by. We suddenly become aware of opportunities a limited love would never have noticed.

Maybe the adventure you are praying for is not going to come to you in the way you think; maybe it awaits discovery through your willingness to take love further today. So let's for the next few pages explore these beautiful verses in Corinthians, which invite us to discover a love that goes beyond.

Beyond Love Is... Patient

Patience is hard enough but a love that is patient is beyond. Patient love is not just waiting but waiting in love; loving in the gap and believing the best. Patient love doesn't watch the clock for the change to happen or insist on things happening in a certain way at a certain time. Think of how patient God's love is towards each one of us. He is patient when we fail, and when we doubt. The patience He expresses visits our life like a reassuring wave of love, bringing us back to shore when we are drifting away with distractions or have become lost or confused by challenges and diversions. Patient love keeps showing up, keeps trusting, keeps holding on. It doesn't press on you its frustration but instead loves you faithfully. Patient love never puts a clamp on your life because you have run out of time. Instead it pays the meter for you to have the time you need with words of affirmation and tenderness that help you rather than hurry you.

The truth is, patient love is often the very thing that gives freedom. It's the fact that love would wait that makes us want to move on. I remember when I was struggling at school in several subjects and my teachers had lost patience with me. I was about to give up because they had given up on me. It wasn't until a friend of our family came and sat with me and patiently went over all the work I couldn't understand that I began to believe I could try again. They had patient love and because they loved me patiently, I progressed eventually.

Today, where is your love in need of more patience? Where has impatience taken over and you are feeling only frustration? Where do you need to stop running the meter of expenses and instead express a love that goes beyond the frustration and moves into a new level of patience? Love that is beyond is patient. You will need that love someday too, so sow now into others the love you will be so grateful to have extended to you in the future.

66

OUR HEART'S CAPACITY IS UNLOCKED BY OUR WILLINGNESS TO BECOME LOVE

BEYOND KIND

Love is kind. It does not envy, it does not boast, it is not proud. It does not dishonour others, it is not self-seeking, it is not easily angered, it keeps no record of wrongs.

1 Corinthians 13:4-5

Beyond Love Is... Kind

Have you ever been on the receiving end of someone's kindness? Do you recall how it made you feel? The way that kindness told you that you matter and that you are seen, the kindness in words spoken that lifted you up and spoke life to your weary soul. Kindness has the ability to remind you of your value and affirm in you the greatness that God daily speaks over you. Kindness changes people and it also creates expectation and awakens possibility.

Where does your kindness need to expand? Maybe you find it easy to speak kind words but struggle to demonstrate that same kindness in actions or maybe you are kind to others but unkind to yourself. Where does you commitment to kindness need to move beyond? Where does it need to stretch so it can reach more people and spread more love? We need more kindness in our schools, workplaces, communities and homes. The kindness that will teach people what real love is and how real love acts.

Jesus was a kind man; when He walked through neighbourhoods, He didn't try to impress people, He loved people and many of the ways He did that was through acts of kindness. It was kindness that caused Him to call the children to Himself when the disciples were dismissing them. It was kindness that noticed the beggar everyone tried to silence and it was kindness that caused Jesus not just to teach multitudes but to then take care of their physical needs by feeding them. Jesus' love was kind and that's what moved people beyond listening into following. Where does this example become your kindness challenge?

Beyond Agenda

Often it is easier to love those who seem to need our love or who are in lack; we can find it harder to express that same depth of love to those who have more than enough or those who we feel a little inferior to. The love that we are called to have is immune from what people do or don't have and it is rooted in loving people for who they are. This love doesn't envy when someone else is prospering. This love is not too proud to humble itself even when it's hard and may feel that love is not returned. The love that goes beyond doesn't advertise its actions, it doesn't need applause or recognition, it is not given to prove a point. This love is beyond the motivation of self.

Where do we need to check the motivation behind our love? Sometimes we can express love because we are wanting to feed some deficiency in our own lives. We can love with an agenda. We hope by giving love in a certain direction, we will be rewarded or embraced, we will gain something that feeds our own soul. Yet a love beyond is given free of any of these returns. If your love has become self-seeking or boastful, if it has become tainted by pride or envy, be willing to remove the things that are making the valve in your heart faulty so that love can flow freely once again. Love from a place of surrender not self, from a place of security not envy.

No-one is immune from feeling annoyed and frustrated, we all get upset but this verse is challenging us to look at how quickly we let go of love and replace it with a poor substitute. If our love doesn't run deep, we can give way to other emotions in times of testing and temptation. How fast do we move from frustration to anger and how long do we keep records of how we have been let down or hurt? Yet beyond love closes the account as it knows it has already received more love than it could ever earn. This love teaches us to not record the wrongs but focus on doing what's right, removing the tab that revenge would like to start. This loves forgives quickly and chooses to forget the hurt that has no place at the table love sets.

It's hard to love beyond the pain but it is possible. It's hard to love when you feel you have been let down but it's that kind of love that moves you beyond. Jesus was a constant source of love and even when people let Him down, He moved on in love. When He was betrayed He forgave, when He was rejected He loved anyway. If Jesus had kept an account of His hurts, He would also have fuel to feed His frustration. Yet Jesus knew, if I live in a place of pain, I can't love with the same passion. His love liberated because His love was not imprisoned by the actions of others.

In Matthew 5:43, Jesus went as far as instructing us that not only should we love those who are hard to love but also we should go beyond and love our enemies. Think about that: the person you would see as an adversary becoming the place you start to express more love. It's the opposite of how we want to respond but what if we decide to let this aspect of our love grow? What if we choose to live in a way that may be costly but is rewarded by discovering a new level of liberty? Remember the Grinch, whose heart was three times smaller than everyone else's? It took a lot of exposure to people he had closed his heart to for that heart to grow and find its true potential.

The scripture goes on to say, if our enemy has taken from us we should gift wrap our coat and give it to them. What love is this? It's beyond love and it's actually one of the greatest discoveries you can make if you want to live a life liberated by love. Where can you work on the things that frustrate you? Where do you need to love more? Is it in a current relationship? Is it in your parenting or marriage? If you want a deeper love then you need shorter accounts, less time spent on what is wrong and more time spent focusing on the One who is love, allowing Him to teach you how to love.

"

PATIENT LOVE KEEPS SHOWING UP, KEEPS TRUSTING, KEEPS HOLDING ON

BEYOND
LIMITS

Love does not delight in evil but rejoices
with the truth. It always protects, always
trusts, always hopes, always perseveres.
Love never fails...
And now these three remain: faith, hope
and love. But the greatest of these is love.

1 Corinthians 13:6-8 & 13

Always is a big word. It's a beyond word. Always asks us to remove the inconsistencies and show a level of reliability that demands much more than we are often prepared to give. Always goes beyond our occasional feelings, our temperamental or circumstantial reactions. It asks us to find a love that is immune from the changing tides of life and love in a way that has a permanent quality about it.

Beyond Love Always... Protects

A love that always protects is a love that jumps first to the role of defender and guardian before it would ever give way to the voices of accuser or judge. It's using our love like a shield, taking it into every situation with us, ready to use it in conversation and action where someone needs defending or supporting. This love that is protective cares about the person more than the opinion. In a world where many are vulnerable, we need more people to understand love that protects, love that shelters, love that provides a safe place even in the midst of the worst storm. We may be good at protecting what we feel is right or what has a value to us but a love that always protects is not restricted by such a criteria. It is reliable, integral and consistent. Where can your voice express a covering of love and protection? What gossip should your love interrupt to protect the person it seeks to pull down? Where can your love speak up for the one who is not given a voice? Where can your love protect what God loves: His people, His church, His family?

Beyond Love Always... Hopes

A love that always hopes challenges us because we all have times when our hopes are unfulfilled. I remember when we went through our infertility journey, this became a very real test. When our hope was on the rollercoaster of tests and doctors reports, when there were so many external factors to our future, finding a love that always hopes became a daily challenge. However, it is possible, in fact it is a game changer, when you understand how to love in a way that hopes always and it is powerful to find a love that can persevere even in the most painful of times.

Beyond Love Always... Perseveres

Love that always perseveres isn't immune from the pain, from the stress of the wait, from the disappointment but its response is set. Like a thermostat in a house, it sets the temperature no matter what the weather outside is doing. Is your love here yet?

CHAPTER TWO

Do you have a love that is so robust it holds in times when your world is shaken? Does your love always choose hope? Does it always stick around long after the butterflies and warm feelings have subsided? This love is not a fairytale love: it's real and robust love that trusts and decides to never give up.

Love isn't passive and it isn't weak. God's way of loving is strong. His love is based on truth and that truth is powerful. Perhaps one of the reasons why we struggle to love extravagantly is found in Matthew 22:9, where we are instructed to love others as we love ourselves. Perhaps you don't know how to love your own life well. Self-love is not being selfish, it's having a confidence in who you are and whose you are. Loving yourself means valuing what God says about you and not allowing wrong words to define and devalue you. I have been through seasons in my journey where I have not loved myself. I have been unhappy about my appearance; I have had personality traits that needed a lot of work; I have had career disappointments. These things can cause us to devalue ourselves, to loathe rather than love who we are. So if loving yourself is the beginning of your beyond journey, then start it now.

The truth is, when we don't love ourselves, we can't love others well. If we don't acknowledge we are worth loving, we are rejecting all God says about us. His love has no limits and there is nothing you can do to make Him love you anymore or any less. That reality is something to rejoice over, real love is something to be celebrated. Let your love be bathed in His light, let it reflect His truth. Be thankful for the depth of a love that went beyond every lie and every evil thing that sought to taint this love. Let the way God loves you shape the truth of how powerful love can be. Say it out loud today: I am fearfully and wonderfully made. I am chosen. I am a child of God. I am loved beyond measure. You are lovely and when you receive this truth, you will love in a whole new way.

We can read these verses as a nice ideal. We can reduce them to just being a passage of scripture we read at weddings or special occasions but these words are some of the most powerful and challenging verses you could ever apply to your life. Love really does change everything and everyone it encounters. These words are your invitation to take love beyond - just imagine if we all choose to embrace it. What if you work on the area you find most challenging and I work on mine? What a gift we would give to ourselves and one another.

Where is that countertop we talked about earlier blocking your love? What ceiling has been put on your heart? It's time to do something that will take that love further. Where can you start to grow your love? What truth can you embrace that will change how you love yourself ? Where can you focus on your love becoming more consistent or indeed more persistent? If God is love, then we can find all the answers and all the examples we need by going back to Him every time. Think how He has loved you when you felt unlovely, loved you when you let Him down, loved you back to health and wholeness. How His love has covered your mistakes and breathed life on your potential. Love is a power we can all unleash and so today, begin to identify where it is time to take your love beyond.

CHAPTER TWO

"

LOVING FROM A PLACE OF SURRENDER MEANS REMOVING ANY OTHER AGENDA

BEYOND
LOVE

THE CHALLENGE

SEE IT

First things first, as we have discovered, we can't love others well until we are loving ourselves well. So, the challenge this month is to love yourself well in words and deeds. That will mean taking a good long and honest look at the way you speak about yourself, the way you think about yourself and the way you treat yourself. So let's start going beyond in your love by seeing the areas where you need to love yourself a little better. That might look like examining your schedule and seeing where you can give yourself some time. We can all say we have no time but the truth is, you are often the last person who you give that time too. Journal below ways in which you can make room for doing some things you love. Maybe you need to look at taking up a new hobby, buying the shoes, eating the cupcake. Make notes on the ways you need to see yourself differently so you can love yourself and others more completely.

SAY IT

Sometimes we wait for words of love to be spoken to us yet the most powerful words of love have already been spoken over us. Where do you need to start to read and speak over your life the word of God? Take some time to meditate and confess His unconditional and unchanging love toward you. Take time to devote yourself to scripture that speaks about the way God sees you. Write the verses down, put them on your mirror and read them out loud everytime you see them. Words that affirm you and build you up in love, words that encourage you. Don't worry if at first it feels strange, after a few days it will be natural to you. Instead of complaining about your appearance or focusing on what you don't like about yourself, say I love myself enough that I am going to receive and walk in that love. What do you need to start to say today?

DO IT

Now you have surrounded yourself with words of love, you're in a better place to start this part of the challenge but don't be fooled, it won't be easy. The challenge is to love the person you currently find the hardest to love. Maybe that's someone you know really well, a family member or someone you were once close to. Maybe it's a person who has deeply offended you or someone from a very different background to yours. The Bible isn't asking you to allow people back into your world that could bring harm to you, but it is asking you to learn to love in a way that stops the harm from carrying on inside of you. Loving those who may have become an enemy or are difficult to love requires forgiveness and wisdom but the process of letting love replace hurt or even hate is powerful.

When you have identified your hard to love person or if you're brave, persons, write their name(s) down and pray for them everyday. Pray for blessing in their life. You won't feel like it at first but this love is beyond feelings. When they come to mind, instead of harboring negative thoughts, think something positive, perhaps even say or do something about it. This is the way to become free. Your aim is not to make this person your best friend, it's for you to be able to love regardless of what their response will be. Think of something you could do this month to express this love in their direction. It doesn't need to be an action that you add your name to; you could do something anonymously but the act will itself become a point of freedom for you as you choose to love beyond.

_____
_____
_____
_____
_____
_____
_____
_____
_____
_____
_____
_____
_____

NOTES

CHAPTER THREE

BEYOND FREE

BEYOND FREE

Jesus replied, "Very truly I tell you, everyone who sins is a slave to sin. Now a slave has no permanent place in the family, but a son belongs to it forever. So if the Son sets you free, you will be free indeed."

John 8:34-36

This verse is one we often quote and its truth is way more powerful than most comprehend. God wants us to know that we are not just free but we are 'free indeed'. The freedom that Christ paid the highest price for is beyond any limitation the enemy would try and intimidate our lives with. We are called to a freedom that goes beyond fear, beyond doubt, beyond our failings and beyond circumstances. This freedom is a gift that we are given and yet often it can stay only partially opened. We can allow shame and regret or the opinions and decisions of others, to keep us from unpacking the full gift that this freedom was given to become.

I watched such a sad documentary about the journey of a young elephant. He had been taken from his home, where he once roamed freely, and relocated to an enclosure. Slowly but surely the elephant was reprogrammed to live in a way that served his newly found containment. This animal was taught a behaviour that was far from his original nature, he was led to believe he was powerless, when the truth was he had the power to stamp on the very people who were making him feel weak. As the elephant grew and his spirit was broken, he was taught to perform as a circus animal and accept peanuts as a reward for his compliance. The animal became so conditioned by his environment that when he was too large to fit in a cage, his owners simply replaced the prison of bars for a chain around his ankle. He could have simply snapped the chain with one move but he didn't stray because he had forgotten the power he possessed. There was no cage to contain him and though the exterior offered freedom, the internal behaviour of the powerful animal remained powerless and imprisoned. How sad to see such greatness live with such smallness. How terrible that an animal that was made to run free had been trained to live contained and controlled.

How much of our lives can we see reflected in that elephant? Where have we allowed an exchange to take place of the freedom we have been given for a life that is bound and contained? We all have so much more of this freedom to explore: the freedom to dream, to believe, the freedom to ask, to be forgiven, to be loved, the freedom to trust and to try.

In order to live in that freedom we have to start to acknowledge some of the bars in our self-inflicted prison and in order to become free we have to also identify areas where we, like that elephant, are actually holding the key. We may like to blame others or our circumstances for our restricted living and of course some people can control and contain our lives, but we must not allow these things to excuse or paralyse us. We have a key that is able to unlock and liberate. The key that is within us is the One who came to give us freedom. If the One who is greater is living on the inside, then there is no bar or chain He cannot break.

Passport To Freedom

Freedom is a passport that you are given when you say yes to Christ. He gives you a brand new identity in Him and with that a passport to explore new possibilities and to go to new destinations that sin wouldn't allow. He stamps the passport with the seal of His blood that paid the price and He then entrusts that passport into your hands. The thing about a passport however is you have to use it in order to feel its benefit. I think we expect this freedom to work without us but God has designed our whole relationship with Him to be one that involves participation. He has given you the passport and now it's for you to be willing to go into some new territory and explore. He wants you to go to the place called forgiveness and He wants you to travel into the life called acceptance. He has already given you the passport to move to the land called liberty, where people's control over you is replaced with God's leading and guidance before you.

I travel a lot and so I know how valuable a passport is. I was recently given my American passport but it was only my willingness to take on a new citizenship that qualified me for this level of access. Freedom is a journey you must keep being willing to take. You may have freedom because you have received forgiveness but what about travelling to the land of freedom where you forgive? What about travelling beyond where you can see and finding a new land of not just being free but free indeed? Maybe you have allowed your freedom to take you as far as trusting God but what about the freedom that allows you to let another be trusted with your love? What about the freedom you have access to, where you tell your story and by doing this leave the place where you have become landlocked by shame and regrets.

Recently as a family we were heading to Africa on a mission trip. We were so excited to step into this new adventure of bringing freedom to many children's lives through a brand new project we had committed to help establish with the charity Compassion.

Months of planning had gone into this trip, meetings and agendas and plans on both sides of the world so that these few days would have maximum impact. We got to the airport early, eager to get going and then the most dreaded moment played out as my husband went to hand over all our passports, four family members and yep, only three passports. My husband had packed my American passport instead of his British one. It didn't matter how much we had done to get to this point or how great the plans were, no passport, no access.

The passport was the way to get to the next thing and the same is true with our freedom in Christ. You have to take it to the border control and show your freedom, put it under the nose of the circumstances that are seeking to control you. You need to know your freedom gives you access that allows you to say not to control and shame. It allows you to pass the fear of failure and go into a new land called grace and mercy.

Every time we leave our passport in the drawer called disappointment or hurt, we deny ourselves access to a new place of departure for a fresh destination and God encounter. Your passport needs to be retrieved from where you last left it because to be free indeed means you have to be willing to travel beyond where you have previously been.

"

THERE IS NOTHING ABOUT THAT SMALL LIFE THAT SUITS YOU

EXPLORING
OUR FREEDOM

About midnight Paul and Silas were praying and singing hymns to God, and the other prisoners were listening to them. Suddenly there was such a violent earthquake that the foundations of the prison were shaken. At once all the prison doors flew open, and everyone's chains came loose.

Acts 16:25-26

Remember when God told Moses he was going to go and set the children of Israel free? God would use Moses as the passport to freedom for millions of people. Moses was hesitant but he knew he had to be willing to go where fear was trying to forbid him. His yes wasn't just about his freedom but about the freedom of many more lives. The same is true for us. Our willingness to live free is never just about us, it's about all those attached to us. Moses went and faced Pharaoh and secured freedom for God's people. He came to the Red Sea and lifted his passport, the staff God had used to show His power, and God parted the waves. His willingness to place his feet in the water and believe there was a life awaiting the children of Israel beyond the border was the first step for all those who would follow in his footsteps.

We must never lose the awareness that our freedom will ultimately become the gift we give to those around us. When we find freedom, we attain more hope and liberty for the generations that follow. I have met people in their twenties and thirties who don't have a passport; they didn't see the need because in their upbringing, travel was never something they were exposed to or encouraged to explore. Their parents did not travel and so now they see no reason to get a passport and travel themselves. We can do the exact same thing to one another spiritually when we don't go beyond; we keep the barricade there for another generation. Imagine if the great explorers of our time had remained in the corner of the world they already knew. We would know nothing of the new lands just waiting to be discovered. Your willingness to explore becomes someone else's passport to new possibilities.

Moses, when he parted the sea, was also presenting the gift of freedom to every single one of those who had lived for years in slavery and hardship. Before them now was the opportunity to explore, to live in the promised land where they could build not under the bonadage of a slave owner but freely for the future of their own families. Yet sadly we know how the story ends; the incredible gift they were given became a gift that was wasted, as they circled and circled in a desert not willing to take the next step to not just be free but live free indeed. They allowed a negative report to keep them out of the future they had already been given. They allowed the fears of a few people to rob them of their freedom. When you allow the volume on your fears to be greater than that on your future, you will always back away from the beyond kind of freedom that God has for you. Stepping into the new requires a determination to not listen to the enemy, to know he is a liar and to understand there is nothing about that small life that suits you.

CHAPTER THREE

Beyond freedom is when your fear no longer gets to be your tour operator. When your chains no longer choose your chorus. We will often still have to deal with things that can imprison us. Lack can limit, people can prohibit, seasons can stifle. We are not immune from the things that can make us feel like we are locked down and yet living with beyond freedom means you have a complete transformation in how you view your chains. If we serve the chain breaker then we don't need to overemphasise the problem, we need to just live from our place of freedom.

Paul and Silas were bound and yet they were free; they were in chains and yet their hearts were not contained. Their circumstances were not choosing their confession. Their words were carefully chosen because they knew they already had freedom. We all too often live free when things are going our way and then when we have something that we feel limits us, we change our language and the way we live. If these men of God could sing in chains, why can't we? If they could praise in a prison, so can we. They knew they had the key to freedom, no prison guard could control what God was already in control of.

Sometimes we over-complicate things, we make our situations more bound because of our own behaviour. Often when I travel I put my jewellery in one small bag, only to find at the other end of the journey when I unpack the necklaces have become intertwined and now, instead of being nicely arranged, they are twisted together. The chains have become a mess, but I don't at that point throw the necklaces away as I know they have too much value to discard. Instead I untwist what has become twisted. Our attitude to the chains we are in will either make the situation worse or it will start to bring release. Signing in a prison is the opposite to what we may feel like doing but it's the key that unlocks the situation. It's the confession that loosens the chain. Freedom that goes beyond sings to the barren areas and praises in the prison. Today, where can you start to do things that are the equivalent of singing in captivity? The enemy may try and intimidate you but you have a freedom song within you. It's already been paid for so don't just think free, live free, speak free, sing free.

INCREASE
REQUIRES
DECREASE

As Jesus started on His way, a man ran up to Him and fell on his knees before Him. "Good teacher," he asked, "what must I do to inherit eternal life?"... Jesus looked at him and loved him. "One thing you lack," He said. "Go, sell everything you have and give to the poor, and you will have treasure in heaven. Then come, follow Me." At this the man's face fell. He went away sad, because he had great wealth.

Mark 10:17-20

We can think we are free indeed and not even realise we have some areas where we are still bound. Going back to the story of our friend the elephant, he may have thought that once the bars had been removed, he was free and yet he was still living like a captive. I have met some people who are living their lives for God and yet have areas that are on lock down. Those who serve wholeheartedly but live fearfully, those who speak boldly, but live stingily. They have used the passport to become free in certain ways but other areas are yet to be discovered. The rich young ruler had so many things going for him but when he asked Christ for true freedom, he was given an instruction that revealed he actually didn't want to be fully free. His possessions had become his prison. His ability to make wealth had become a chain to his freedom. Instead of releasing, he wanted to hold on.

If we are not careful, we can think we are free, even look and act free, yet like a puppet that may move and dance, we have allowed our freedom to have strings attached and those strings can be placed in many different hands. Free indeed living means we cut all the strings off our life and give God full control. For this young ruler, he didn't want to give up control of his resources and therefore he remained bound in an area where Jesus was trying to offer him true freedom. Jesus was not intending to make the man poor when He asked him to give away his wealth. He was trying to lead him to a place of true riches, where being free enough to release ultimately moves your life to the most incredible place of increase. Don't allow what you have to restrict what you do and where you go. If God is our source, then we can live free of the fear of losing the resources of friends or popularity. Freedom that lives beyond is freedom in every area, from oppression to possessions.

Jesus would tell His disciples regularly - just go and don't take all those things with you that will become a hindrance to you. Some of the release we need is from the good as well as the bad. Don't allow the approval of others to become the border you can't pass, don't battle with a willingness to be generous, thinking release will mean decrease when actually the real truth is, release brings increase. When things have no control over you, that's when you can live with a beyond freedom. Elijah asked the widow making her last meal to share her food with a passing prophet. In that moment she had a choice: is my freedom in what I have or is my freedom in what I don't understand? Real freedom at times makes no sense but that's why it's called free indeed.

CHAPTER THREE

Free To Be Me

Living beyond free often means embracing the adventure of liberating all God has made you to be. I am sure no one reading this is a people pleaser or at times wants to prove someone wrong. I am sure you live immune from doubting yourself or living someone else's version of you. Just in case you are still reading and may find this helpful, let's remember that to be really free, you have to be really you and I have to be really me. Masks are not sustainable, a false identity will not get you across into the land of freedom.

When we were stuck at the airport with one passport missing, even though Steve and I shared our last name, even though I could vouch for who he was, they wouldn't allow him access until they saw his actual ID. Real freedom can't be found with someone else's passport. Just because our group have made the booking does not mean our whole group will make the crossing. Even babies need passports, however unsure, uncertain, young and inadequate we may feel, we must make our own journey when it comes to exploring the depths and lengths of God's freedom for each of our lives.

This became a test that Gideon had to take. When God said go and take the land, go and get your freedom, the invitation was for Gideon to step into a new level of living. He had to stop hiding and start advancing but he wasn't free in who he was. When the angel came and found him in the winepress, Gideon identified himself as weakest of the weak, my family are weak, I am weak. His identity was not based in who God said he was but in his family history and who that made him believe he was. Gideon had an identity crisis and it was stopping him from finding freedom. In Judges 6 we see God's simple reply: Gideon, the only way you get free is by going in the strength you have. God was teaching Gideon, you don't wait to become someone else and then find freedom, you go in the strength you have now; take that passport to the border of insecurity and face the boundary of inferiority. Free indeed means I am free to be me. Gideon's weakness was not able to unlock his freedom, it was only his willingness that could do that.

So where do you need, like Gideon, to explore your freedom by going in the strength you have? Where you are free indeed, you are very aware of the lack but you are committed to taking the step beyond anyway.

When you are free you are aware others could do it better but you do it anyway. Like David when he faced Goliath, you take the best you have got, even if it's just a stone and throw it at what's between you and all that's to come. Being free indeed means embracing the freedom that comes by being free to be me.

What a waste it would be to live in the corner of our freedom when we have been given access to so much more. What a travesty if we were to say we were free but live as if we were bound. Where is it time to move your freedom beyond? Do you need to forgive to be free? Step out and be free, let things go, move beyond the voices that would keep you small and make the choices that will move your life, your faith and your freedom forward. Let's be those who know the Son has set us free and determine to make sure we live free indeed.

CHAPTER THREE

"

YOU HAVE A FREEDOM SONG WITHIN YOU - SO SING!

BEYOND
FREE

THE CHALLENGE

SEE IT

This month the challenge is to live in new areas of the freedom that is already yours to possess. In order to do so, you are going to have to change some of the ways you see your life. Identify areas where you are allowing either fear, a sense of doubt or even shame or guilt to keep you contained. Whatever the false prison you have accepted, decide this month to do a prison break. Maybe you have an area where you need to untangle what God never intended to be complicated, so that the chains you have justified can be removed and you can live unbound. Stop the behaviour that is keeping you down, the negative thought pattern, the containing company. Start to do the things that move you from bound to free. Where do you need to get your passport out and get over border control? Maybe you feel free in certain areas but where has your freedom not fully travelled yet? Identify a list of places you want to go, places only freedom can take you and start to see you have the access to move beyond the border where your fear is keeping you captive.

SAY IT

Once you have identified the areas where you need to see more freedom, you now need to plan a course of action that will make that freedom possible. Write three headings:

Think Free
Speak Free
Act Free

Then think of ways in each one of these areas that you can begin to unlock your life. For example, your sticking point may be generosity and you want to become free from the chains of possessions. Where can you stop thinking all the time about what you do or don't have and instead start to be appreciative of things you have maybe overlooked? Perhaps you need freedom from an area of regret or shame and so need to examine where you need to forgive and be forgiven. What do you need to stop dwelling on so you can start gaining freedom and move on? Write down your area and write what confession and actions need to change.

_____
_____
_____
_____
_____
_____
_____
_____
_____
_____
_____
_____
_____
_____
_____
_____
_____
_____

DO IT

Attaining freedom is a process that will require commitment so don't try and rush past this point. Maybe the action you need to add for freedom to become possible is accountability, maybe its going for counselling; it may be an area of addiction that needs to be broken. Be brave and begin to make some decisions that will change your life in the area where you need breakthrough so you can not just be free but free indeed.

NOTES

CHAPTER FOUR

BEYOND
TIDY

BEYOND
TIDY

So Naaman went with his horses and chariots and stopped at the door of Elisha's house. Elisha sent a messenger to say to him, "Go, wash yourself seven times in the Jordan, and your flesh will be restored and you will be cleansed." But Naaman went away angry and said, "I thought that he would surely come out to me and stand and call on the name of the Lord his God, wave his hand over the spot and cure me of my leprosy."

2 Kings 5:9-11

We have all done it, well at least I have. You know people are coming over but time seems to be running away from you and you need to get things in order and quickly. So you start grabbing what should have been put away hours ago and stuffing things in cupboards, pushing items into drawers that are already bursting. You don't have time to sort out the pile of clothes you were meaning to get to so you just put the whole lot in the laundry basket. A few frenzied moments later you have created the illusion of order. The place looks nice and tidy and only you know the truth.

We can have the same approach in many areas of our lives. We want things to be tidy but we don't take the time to do the real work necessary, so we simply keep stuffing issues in the drawer or living with a level of order that works on the surface but would be embarrassing if anyone was to open those cupboards. We hide behind routine to keep things moving rather than facing things that will demand more of us. When we are asked if we are ok or we need any help we say 'I'm fine' and hope that the person asking will know that answer was not an invitation to any further enquiries.

Where has the 'I'm fine', the surface tidy up of our lives meant that we are now living in a way that has limited our own breakthrough? Where have we hidden so many issues that now it's time for a clear out? Often we can find we are restricting our own progress because we have allowed our routine, our business as usual approach, to stifle us. God wants you to let Him in, He already knows what's in those cupboards, the issues that have been hidden under the bed, He knows when the 'I'm fine' is fake. He wants to help you sort out the things you have been ignoring or avoiding. He has better for you than just ok, He is a limitless God and therefore fine is not in His plan for your life. In order to get beyond tidy in any area of our lives, we have to be willing to do some things that you may feel are embarrassing.

Beyond Embarrassed

The story of Naaman is one that we can all learn from. Our issue may not be ill health but we can still share his level of discomfort at anyone knowing what he was really struggling with. Naaman had a reputation of strength and yet he was hiding a painful weakness. It took a servant girl, without her master's permission and risking her job and comfortable living arrangements, to call on the prophet and say, everything is not ok. Elisha went to the house of this soldier who was known for fighting on the battlefield but now would need to accept help to fight a very different battle a lot closer to home. Naaman's body was covered in leprosy and no suit of armour could help him win this fight.

Elisha, however, made a very uncomfortable request of Naaman. If he wanted to be healed, he needed to go and dip in the river Jordan seven times. At this suggestion, Naaman, who wanted to keep up appearances, was outraged. His embarrassment factor had been found and he was offended that he would have to go and do something that he deemed was so beneath him. Yet in order for Naaman to have wholeness, for him to move beyond just being ok to being fully well, he was going to have to allow this miracle to take place God's way. There was something about every one of those dips he took that moved his life beyond where his tidy would allow. The one who gave orders was now following orders; the one who was saying he was fine was now seen to be anything but fine. The water was not only washing the disease off him but it was also washing away the barriers that he had built within himself. Naaman had a choice: get worse or be clean. The difference was not in God's ability but in Naaman's willingness to move beyond his embarrassment and need for control and let God do the miracle His way.

Sometimes we just need to be taken past our embarrassment factor. I have discovered God likes to be that embarrassing parent. He wants to overwhelm you with love. He wants to shout affirmation over you. He wants to speak to your potential. Imagine being at your sports day as a child and God is there as your father. I don't think He would sit on the sidelines, He would be that dad that was cheering for you, taking photos and documenting how brilliantly you were doing. When you were unsure, He would be cheering as if you had already won the gold. Why? Because God wants you to be all He made you to be and that goes way beyond just being fine. God loves to bless you beyond, He wants to move you from enough to showing you He has more than enough. Where would you like to say, no it's ok, I'm fine, it's enough, so that no fuss is made? Is it when it comes to someone asking if they can serve you in a certain way? Is it helping you with your children or finances? Where do you feel uncomfortable?

I had to learn this lesson the hard way; I was the master at saying 'I'm fine'. I wanted to do everything myself and not be a bother to anyone else. I remember once carrying several very heavy bags up a large flight of stairs and someone simply asking, can I help? My answer: no, I'm fine. Well five seconds later one of the bags tore and the contents dispersed in many different directions. It was like God ripped the bag open to teach me a lesson. I wasn't fine, I had way too heavy a load and I needed some help. As people started to pick up my possessions that were rolling down the staircase I was even more embarrassed as I was forced to acknowledge I did not have the situation covered. Where in your world are you using fine as the door stop to going beyond? Where is your embarrassment blocking your blessing? God sent His Son so that you could see how far and how lavish His love is for you. Don't let embarrassment oppose His favour and shrink your world.

CHAPTER FOUR

"

*ON THE DAY WHEN
THE DARKNESS SEEMS
TO BE CLOSING IN,
YOU STILL HAVE JESUS
IN THE BOAT*

BEYOND
PEACE

Leaving the crowd behind, they took Him along, just as He was, in the boat. There were also other boats with Him. A furious squall came up, and the waves broke over the boat, so that it was nearly swamped. Jesus was in the stern, sleeping on a cushion. The disciples woke Him and said to Him, "Teacher, don't You care if we drown?" He got up, rebuked the wind and said to the waves, "Quiet! Be still!" Then the wind died down and it was completely calm.

Mark 4:36-39

In an effort to stay in control and keep our lives tidy, we often work hard to make sure nothing disturbs the peace we have established. We avoid the awkward conversation as we don't want any conflict. We stay away from the situation that may mean we have to face things directly because our tidy lives often have a very fragile peace attached to them. To go deeper would be to take us beyond what our current peace can sustain. Just under the surface of our tidy is a level of messy that we know may cause unrest and so we resist the deeper clean for the sake of keeping the current order.

Many of us are familiar with the verse in Philippians 4 that speaks of the peace that transcends understanding and yet we have never really discovered it because to do so would mean tidy giving way to messy. What does a peace that passes understanding look like and how do we move from a place of getting by, of holding on to routines for our security, to a peace that's beyond? I think a lot of times our peace is too fragile. It can easily be shattered or disturbed. It's like when you're relaxing in a swimming pool, you are just enjoying the peace and quiet and the sun and the water and then a child (or an over enthusiastic adult!) shows up from nowhere and dive bombs into the pool. All of a sudden, the scene of tranquility has been disturbed by someone yelling, 'cannon ball!'. I think that's what an ok peace looks like, at anytime a break in our routine, a circumstance or a relational situation could drop into the serenity and seriously disturb the peace we are trying to stay afloat in. Building our peace on our surroundings results in a peace that's circumstantial. What about discovering the kind of peace that isn't just fine, it's fierce? The kind of peace that makes no sense because it passes understanding. The bad news doesn't change it, the unforeseen circumstances don't shatter it. This peace holds when others leave and it is not depleted when life's demands get greater. This peace is not an ok peace, it's a beyond type of peace.

Jesus modelled this kind of peace in the storm. The disciples were rowing the boat and He was sleeping; the storm came and the peaceful scene changed and so did the disciples demeanor. Panic replaced peace and what was once steady was now seriously unstable. Yet the Prince of Peace was in the boat and He was sleeping because a peace that passes understanding chooses its response instead of reacting to everything around it. Jesus was demonstrating how strong peace can be. He slept in the storm because He knew the storm had no power over Him. He slept because He knew the wind and waves would die down. He slept in the storm because He wasn't surprised at its occurrence. We need to discover this same peace.

Why do we freak out when things go off plan, when our tidy gets messed up? Why are we panicking when the storm shows up? We need to learn how to remain calm and remove the shock factor by digging deeper and making our peace one that is weatherproof.

When I was in the USA recently, I was sat outside on the front porch of a home watching everyone running around while I relaxed. When I enquired why people seemed to be clearing their front porch rather than reclining on it, I was informed that they were heeding a storm warning. They were planning now so they didn't panic later. Our peace needs to act in the same manner; instead of allowing it to constantly take a hit, we need to tie our peace down in advance so that when the storm comes we are prepared. The disciples only needed to focus on who was in the boat instead of the wind and waves and their peace would have remained.

When you are constantly distracted, you are continually disturbing your peace, so it can't be based on what you can control, manage, comprehend, it has to go beyond. Your peace cannot be attached to your job, income, friends or health. The only way your peace moves beyond its fragile state is by being centred in Christ. It's a peace that says, if it all fails, He doesn't; if they all leave, He won't; if it's all lost, He isn't. Jesus is in the boat in the good and bad weather and He is at peace. You have to say, I don't get it but I am not going to stress about it; I am going to replace my worry with His peace. Don't give your peace away to people who will misuse it. Don't put your peace in possessions, they can't sustain it. Don't let your peace be fragile: anchor it into God.

If our Saviour is the Prince of Peace, then we should not settle for anything less than the best. We don't have a restricted supply, it's available in abundant measure. Peace communicates with certainty, it does not allow doubt in the dialogue because doubt is a peace stealer. If you have a peace that is beyond then when doubt asks you to converse about all the things that could happen, peace changes the conversation. It doesn't talk about what could be, it talks about what has been. Peace speaks fluently about God's faithfulness and recalls quickly His goodness. Peace does not enter a pointless discussion, it saves its breath as it knows to swim in the struggle requires strength and that strength is a peace that goes beyond. So stop saying 'I'm fine' if your mind is frantic and your peace is shattered into a thousand pieces. Fight for that peace that is promised, work on it until it is waterproof and gain the kind of peace He said was yours for the taking, the peace that passes understanding.

BEYOND
JOY

"I am the gate; whoever enters through Me will be saved. They will come in and go out, and find pasture. The thief comes only to steal and kill and destroy; I have come that they may have life, and have it to the full. I am the Good Shepherd. The Good Shepherd lays down His life for the sheep."

John 10:9-11

The problem with living in a way that is uniform and tidy is we resist extremes. We would rather take what's manageable than explore what we potentially cannot control. Yet the God we serve does extreme: extreme peace, extreme blessing - He is over the top good. The Bible tells us that the life He wants us to have is not just good, it's abundant, overflowing life in all its fullness. There is no keeping tidy an overflowing life; no matter how much you try to contain it, its very nature defies restriction. Where His abundant life has become significantly reduced to a manageable flow, we need to start exercising more flexibility.

One of the places we often stop the overflow is in the area of our joy. We deny ourselves what we feel may be too much or unnecessary, yet in restricting our joy we also restrict our strength because the Bible tells us that joy is strength. When did we become joyless? When did we stop seeing the funny side of things? I have heard people eloquently justify the absence of joy in their life by saying, I am just not that type of person, I don't express myself that way. 'I'm fine' can become a facade for I'm joyless, I'm no fun.

The Bible says the exact opposite when it comes to this subject. Not only is joy connected to strength but we should have a joy unspeakable. Wow, that is definitely beyond 'I'm fine'. What does that even look like? It makes me think of those times when you laugh so hard no sound comes out, when you are laughing so deep, you are crying and almost not breathing at the same time. Maybe you have never laughed like that before. Well maybe it's time you did. Have you heard the quote, laughter is the best medicine? Well, that's from the book of Proverbs. God knows laughter soothes the soul, helps change our perspective and our whole countenance. Jesus is the joy sent to the world. What about you? Is that how people describe you?

God is able in every area of your life to turn the enemy's schemes to defeat you into a dance floor of victory. In Isaiah 61, we are told that the Spirit of God can turn our mourning into dancing, a garment of praise instead of a spirit of despair. The thing about beyond joy is its source is not natural, it's spiritual, it's a dimension beyond. It's the spirit of God that revives and energises. Beyond joy comes when we start to see things correctly. This kind of joy has a way of giving you a perspective shift and instead of seeing the worst it leads your eyes to see the outcome that will become the victory song. It says that Jesus, for the joy set before Him, was able to endure the cross. How could He look at the cross and find joy? Jesus could have seen the pain but He went beyond that and searched for the joy that was your salvation and mine. The joy was freedom to every captive soul; the joy was being reunited with His Father. That is a joy that is beyond: a joy that is steadfast and strong.

The truth is we are called to not just have a safe life but to have an abundant life, that enjoys the depths of His love and the generosity of His grace. A life that delights in His goodness and His favour, that is grateful for His unmerited kindness. One of the ways the enemy keeps us from this life is by causing us to forget just how blessed we are. He is hoping when you get up and start the routine of your day, you forget that new mercy is there and that when you are feeling low, you won't remind yourself of God's overwhelming love. He wants the problems you face to distract you but the truth is, you are abundantly blessed. Complacency is a thief and it will steal your best life out of your hands if you let it. The way we encounter our abundant life is not by going anywhere but by waking up right where we are. That's why Psalm 103 reminds us to "forget not all His benefits".

I recently did a clear out in my son's bedroom; it was time to go beyond tidy. He had so much stuff but no space to put it. We had filled every drawer and even under the bed was full of boxes of things we had tidied away, hoping out of sight would be out of mind. The problem with boxes of stuff is that when anything new arrives in our life, we have no room to accommodate it. Often we are asking for more when if we would just go deeper, we would see we have so much more than we realise. That was the conclusion we came to when we were tidying the room; it led to hours of discovery of things he had forgotten. He had Lego that was not fully constructed, a remote control car he thought he had outgrown but was actually keen to take for another spin. Suddenly my son became grateful all over again for things he had overlooked and didn't know he had.

The beyond life commits to an awareness of His overwhelming goodness so when you are tempted to say you don't have enough, you see all around His more than enough. Don't be so quick to tidy away your provision and forget about the way in which God has answered.

Get out the box of blessing and recount the ways He has been faithful and you will soon find that the God who was there in the past will be there in the current season too. The faithfulness of God has marked and guided every aspect of your life; it is brimming with abundance. Perhaps it's time to update your status from ok to above and beyond blessed.

Beyond tidy is not about ignoring where things are not so good, it's not pretending you don't need help, in fact it's the opposite. It's understanding that on the day when the darkness seems to be closing in, you still have Jesus in the boat. It's weatherproofing your soul so that your peace is not in people, position or possessions, but in the Prince of Peace. Move your life beyond the sticking point of your embarrassment, past the awkwardness of your ok, and let God take you into wide open spaces where joy and faith and abundance overwhelm lack, complacency and inhibitions. So go ahead, the next time someone asks if you're ok, answer in a beyond way. The next time you are tempted to stuff things in the drawer to keep up appearances, just say excuse the mess, I'm a work in progress. Don't allow the need for order to limit you but instead risk the embarrassment and step beyond. The more times we do, the more we help those around us say, I believe God has something beyond for my life too.

CHAPTER FOUR

"

*GOD IS ABLE
IN EVERY AREA
OF YOUR LIFE TO
TURN THE ENEMY'S
SCHEME TO DEFEAT
YOU INTO A DANCE
FLOOR FOR YOUR
VICTORY*

BEYOND
TIDY

THE CHALLENGE

SEE IT

Where is it your routine to say 'I'm fine'? Where is it your habit to tidy away instead of facing the issue? The first part of moving beyond tidy is having the courage to see what you are hiding. So challenge yourself this month to identify an area where you are stuck in a rut, accepting a circumstance to keep your life tidy when really, it needs to change. Is it in your marriage, your mental health, your financial situation, how you handle your kids? Maybe there's a few things; be honest with yourself and with God. If you can identify the behaviour, you can then plan to move beyond.

SAY IT

Now the challenge is, when someone asks you about that area you have identified, and they will, you are not allowed to reply with 'I'm fine'. You have to start to be more honest about the situation. So if someone says, are you ok with the kids, you need to find a different reply. Perhaps mention you could do with some help, that you need an evening without them or you actually need some advice. Change the conversation and by doing so you will open up some new possibilities for you and for those caught up in your routine too. In the area where you are living at just ok, begin to study God's word and write down where He says you can move beyond so you can start to say it too.

DO IT

Where is your spiritual life just managing rather than overflowing? Where are you keeping things so tidy that you are actually restricting access to your blessing: is it your joy, your peace, your faith? Challenge yourself this month in two areas to go deeper and find what is waiting for you. So if your peace is fragile, plan where you can make it waterproof. If you are often confrontational, plan how you can remove yourself from these situations that challenge you peace and instead, find the peace that passes understanding. If you often see the negatives in life, plan a way to bring joy unspeakable into your day. This month, the challenge isn't just to change your confession but also to change the things you are accepting so you can move beyond the tidy into the overflowing life that God wants for you.

NOTES

CHAPTER FIVE

BEYOND ASK

BEYOND
ASK

God can do anything, you know—far
more than you could ever imagine or
guess or request in your wildest dreams!
He does it not by pushing us around but
by working within us, His Spirit deeply
and gently within us.

Ephesians 3:20-21 (MSG)

A few years ago, God spoke to me in a very personal way and what He said changed my life forever. He asked me to begin to ask Him for things like a daughter would a father. He challenged me to come to Him not with needs but with the things I desired. This may seem an exciting idea to you but to me it short circuited how I was wired. I began to realise that one of things I was very good at was coming to God on behalf of others. I would pray and seek God for the church, for friends and others facing challenge. I would even be ok at approaching God for needs in my own life, an area where I needed clarity or healing. I didn't ask God for anything that went beyond need.

I realised God was inviting me on a journey of talking to Him differently; instead of thinking He only had pleasure in solving a problem I realised He delighted in also fulfilling desires. The problem was then that I really hadn't thought much about the things my heart desired. I had always thought it was wrong to waste God's time and heaven's resources on things that made no eternal difference. I knew God didn't mind if we lived a life that was blessed. In fact, He wants that for all of us but I felt that the blessing was ok because it had been worked for not given. I was living where I think a lot of us live, in a place of asking for what was most pressing and never asking for what would be a blessing.

God reminded me of the verse in Ephesians where it speaks of how much more God wants to do. God is inviting us all into a very different relationship. He is saying, I am all you need, I have all you need, I am able and willing way beyond what you are asking. God is also provoking a reaction from us as He says, don't you get it? However big you are thinking, I am beyond. However much you think that ask demands, I have way more than that.

I had to adjust not just my ask but also my approach to God as Father. I knew He is Father God, Abba Father, the good good Father yet I began to realise, the last way I related to God was as my father. In my approach He was Saviour first, Lord, King of kings. I was in awe of Almighty God, I loved to bow in reverence at the feet of my Saviour. I was overwhelmed with gratitude at the darling of heaven's sacrifice. Yet I didn't have the same fast response when it came to coming to Him like a daughter would to her father.

The more I have spoken about this, the more I have realised I am not the only one. Maybe some of us don't feel worthy of such an intimate relationship, maybe others have had a bad model of fathering in their life. Maybe the concept seems almost immature and no longer applicable to those who are older and therefore see themselves with less need of a father. Yet I have been wondering if actually the enemy is more invested in keeping this aspect of God's nature from you than any other. For when you know Him as Father, you also acknowledge your own standing as daughter or son. When you don't just sing, I am a child of God, but get a revelation that is your reality, it shifts the way you not only see God but see yourself. You are His sons and daughters. God calls you His, so how and where do you need to align your response?

I thought about my own daughter and son's relationship with my husband, Steve. How they effortlessly know the love of their father and with that have such a confidence to ask him for any and everything. They have an implicit trust that when they ask, not only will their dad hear but he will do all he can to give the best response.

If all my kids ever asked from us as parents was for needs to be met, it would move our relationship from one that was effortlessly natural to one that had become based on practical tasks. Father God wants to hear not just your needs but your dreams, your fears and desires. He wants you to run to Him like a child would to their father. When my daughter was a toddler she would often ask her dad to pick her up and swing her around. She trusted him to catch her when she jumped and carry her when she was weary. God wants that kind of relationship with you and I and in order for that to be possible, we have to move our conversation and interaction beyond what we need to sharing what our hearts' desire.

This challenge from God began a journey that changed my life forever. Suddenly I became the recipient of acts of kindness that had no attachment to any needs, but were so personal to me. They were things no one else would know that my heart desired but my Heavenly Father. It was like God had put me on a crash course of learning that His capacity was way beyond my understanding. I have had surprise anonymous deliveries from God sent divine relationships. I have experienced incredible mind blowing seasons of provision.

Even typing what up until this point I haven't shared with anyone makes me feel a little uncomfortable because it's not that I did anything special. The boast is not about what I have received, the boast is in the God who loves us so much He wants to show that love in ways our own hearts cannot conceive.

I am still on that journey with God of going deeper in what it means to be a daughter, receiving His confidence and courage, discovering just how much He believes in me. Maybe one day this journey I have been on will become a book in itself but for now, I am still taking notes of the kind of living that is on the other side of our restricted asking.

CHAPTER FIVE

"

WHY DO WE ASK SO SMALL WHEN HE IS LORD OF ALL?

BEYOND
RECEIVING

If any of you lacks wisdom, you should ask God, who gives generously to all without finding fault, and it will be given to you. But when you ask, you must believe and not doubt, because the one who doubts is like a wave of the sea, blown and tossed by the wind.

James 1:5-6

Learning to receive is a journey for so many but it is essential because it is part of the way you move your life beyond need. I discovered through this whole process that I was a terrible receiver; if someone complimented me I would deflect it, if they blessed me I would then look for a way to justify it. If they wanted to do something for me I would suggest someone else that needed it more. To receive the beyond blessing of Ephesians, I needed to find an ability for beyond receiving.

Maybe like me you have some faulty thinking: to ask for yourself is selfish, to want God's time in trivial things is unholy. When God says we should come to Him like a child to the father, when He says in Psalm 37 He wants to give us the desires of our hearts, He is not teasing or lying. God is letting you and me know He is ok with our asking, He can handle it.

In James 1 it teaches us the healthy parameters when it comes to how we ask of God. It doesn't say, don't ask, it says, here's a filter for when you're asking. God wants to answer but He doesn't want us to be hurt by answering demands that will cause more harm than good. James says, stop making it difficult, by all means ask, just make sure your motive is correct, manage the motive then go ahead and ask your Father for your miracle.

The instructions in James are exactly the kind of advice we would give our own children if they asked for things driven by greed or were envious of what others had. If they were asking outside of relationship and the things they were requesting were selfish and harmful, then we would also say the motive needs to be addressed before the request can be answered. God doesn't want us to ask small, He simply wants the motivation of our ask to be measured.

So how do you measure your motive? Well a simple way to move your life beyond need but avoid greed is to build your relationship with your Father God. See Him as a good Father and learn to come to Him in that manner. Just as you would not abuse the kindness of those you love dearly, the same is true when we ask God from a place of love and respect. We ask not to abuse His kindness but we ask because we know He wants to bless us.

CHAPTER FIVE

Beyond Answers

Remember the story in the Bible when Solomon was to become king? He had some very big shoes to fill and as he followed in his father David's footsteps he was more aware than ever that he needed to learn how to come to God in his own right, not just as David's son. Solomon's youth could have led him to waste his ask on things that would have no lasting impact. Yet when Solomon had the opportunity to ask God for whatever he wanted in 2 Chronicles 1, he did not waste this moment.

Perhaps he had learnt from his own father David about the kindness of his Heavenly Father. Maybe his dad had told him of how God had been there for him when no one else had, how He had defended and provided for him. Solomon didn't come and ask God for a need that day, instead he went beyond need because he somehow knew God was able to answer far above what others had asked for. His ask was not for selfish needs or temporal gain, His ask was for wisdom and that ask led God to not just answer but beyond answer.

Solomon came to God as a son who was asking his dad for wisdom and that approach meant the Father wanted in return to give the son what he hadn't even requested. Our ability to ask beyond also triggers answers that go beyond. In 2 Kings 4, Elijah came across a widow who was in debt and struggling to survive. He instructed the woman to go and ask her neighbours for jars but he then added, don't just ask for a few jars. Elijah was saying, don't just get what you think you need, go and get more than you think you will need. Elijah knew something the woman was about to discover, that God doesn't respond to need, He responds to the vessels we bring to Him to fill. The oil was going to keep pouring while ever more vessels needed filling. I wonder how many times our asks are like those jars? We have only asked for what we think we need, when we could have been bringing more jars that would have moved our miracle into a realm that is beyond.

God is not broke, He isn't limited, He isn't saving blessings up nor is He trying to teach us a lesson. He is a good good Father and He wants us to come to Him knowing He has all we would ever need.

BEYOND
POSSIBILITIES

I pray that you, being rooted and established in love, may have power, together with all the Lord's holy people, to grasp how wide and long and high and deep is the love of Christ, and to know this love that surpasses knowledge that you may be filled to the measure of all the fullness of God. Now to Him who is able to do immeasurably more than all we ask or imagine, according to His power that is at work within us...

Ephesians 3:17-20

This verse tells us where we need to be rooted and where our hearts should dwell. Where we dwell drives how we ask. If we dwell in self we ask selfishly, if we dwell in need we ask for needs. If we dwell in Him we ask from a place of relationship. Where are you dwelling and how is it shaping your asking? Perhaps you have spent too long dwelling in the problem, it has altered your ask and it's time to go back and dwell in His presence. Where are you rooted, in lack or in longing? Are you rooted in jealousy or envy or are you rooted in love? When you are rooted in your love for Him and His for you, then you rest and you don't panic. Your asking isn't reactionary, it's relational.

We are told in Ephesians of the ways that God loves us - it's a huge love, beyond our understanding. This love wants us to be filled with His fullness, to lack nothing; He delights in answering our requests to Him. We are invited into the ask, assured of the limitless God we serve. With this encouragement, we are instructed to go beyond our needs as He can do more than we can ask, think or imagine.

So what is your beyond ask? Maybe you need to take some time to think about what that ask would look or sound like. Maybe it scares you to even entertain the idea that God wants you to ask big but if you can start to see Him as your Father and come to Him with that posture, you will realise more and more it's not about asking for no reason or asking just because you can. It's the invitation to ask Him for the things that would be a blessing. It may not even be a big thing but for you, the nature of the ask not being about need anymore is a huge step into beyond asking.

In Ephesians, it doesn't just say what we ask needs to increase but that He will also go beyond what we can imagine. For some our imaginations need no help, they are explosive and powerful but for others we don't dare to imagine the best, to imagine the breakthrough. We have restricted our imagination to what we feel is possible and yet this is God saying to us all, imagine away. Beyond need living requires our imaginations to increase to go past the perimeters of our circumstances and imagine new ways of doing things, new relationships, new and never seen before opportunities.

Our imaginations when we were children never needed any encouragement. We imagined worlds beyond the one we lived in, we imagined monsters under the bed, treasure buried in the garden, we imagined audiences for our imaginary plays and circuses. Our imagination gave us friends when we were lonely and an escape from reality. Yet over time our imagination becomes less used and its voice silenced. We think it's silly to imagine and childish to live in a space in our mind that is so far removed from our reality. Little by little we forget the power of our imagination. We need to understand that the possibilities that God wants us to consider are not restricted to this world and to our own ability. He wants you and I to imagine new ideas, new ways of doing things. We need to engage that childlike ability to imagine once more if we are going to get our head over the counter of need and into the possibility of what could be.

Noah must have felt very silly as he imagined what an ark was, even what rain was. He had no reference points for how God was going to use his life. How many of us could imagine animals turning up on our doorstep two by two? I'm not sure Noah could either but his mind had to go beyond reason and he had to imagine an impossibility becoming his reality or he would never have started building the ark.

God doesn't just want you to view your life through what you can achieve or what you may be able to believe. He wants you to imagine way beyond what is comfortable. God is a good Father and it's when we understand that dynamic of our relationship as a child of God that we start to imagine bigger.

Where do you need to get past seeing God as a problem solver to seeing Him as your Father? Where do you need to come as one who is called daughter, child, friend? When you live need driven, it means everything has to be attached to a purpose but as every parent knows in the natural, we don't need a reason to bless our children. We don't do things based on a purpose, we serve and take care of them because we love them. God loves you and He wants to bless you beyond what you can ask, think and imagine.

When was the last time you imagined with your Heavenly Father? He won't be overwhelmed by what you may see, in fact He will, like any good parent, say, is that all you can see? He will stretch your vision to view even greater horizons. God's capacity is not in question, His willingness is without hesitation, so the restriction is at our end.

Imagine for a moment with me: you are standing at the top of a mountain and God is right next to you, holding your hand. You are surveying the incredible horizon in front of you. You can see for miles and the awe of creation is only surpassed by the awe of holding the hand of the Creator. Now imagine your Father squeezing your hand and asking you, where do you want to go, what do you want to do? You would realise you have so many options and so much space, all the daily challenges would fade away as you imagined a whole new level of conversation. That's what God wants to invite you and I into: mountain top conversations. The valley will still be there but God doesn't want you to live there. He wants you to move to this beyond place with Him and from there to start again to see a new way of living.

"

*THAT'S WHAT GOD
WANTS TO INVITE
YOU AND I INTO:
MOUNTAIN TOP
CONVERSATIONS
SO YOUR VALLEYS
HAVE THE RIGHT
PERSPECTIVE*

BEYOND
ASK

THE CHALLENGE

SEE IT

This month, before you make your ask, you need to think about how you approach God. Do you see Him as your Father and see yourself as His daughter? Perhaps you never felt fathered or were told never to ask for things. God wants to help you, heal you. He wants the wrong image of father to be replaced by the true image of what a father's heart is. He loves you, adores you and wants to bless and prosper you. Start to see yourself as daughter, not servant – work on how you see yourself and allow God to show you how He sees you too.

SAY IT

Now that you can see God as your Father, how can you start talking to Him in this way? What does a father and daughter conversation sound like to you? Try calling Him Father when you pray, knowing that your voice is a sound He loves to hear. You are His daughter and He only wants good things for you. Be mindful this month of the places in the word where His Father heart is revealed, study it and lean into it as His daughter.

DO IT

Now you've addressed how you see and speak to your Heavenly Father, you can make your ask. What can you ask God your Father for this month that may not be a need being filled but instead just a longing fulfilled? There is a difference between asking for what is necessary and asking for what is just His blessing. Remember Jabez in 1 Chronicles when he said, God, I'm asking you to bless me and enlarge me. God didn't seem to mind his request for more and He won't mind your request either. So think about a blessing you would like to ask from your Father and go ahead and make your ask. Still not sure? Consider Caleb's daughter who asked for not just the lower springs but the upper too in Joshua 15. She knew she had favour with her father and so she asked a beyond ask. God is an also God. So don't feel guilty that your ask means someone else won't get blessed. God is more than able to answer all His kids. Dream, believe and maybe for the first time, go to your Father and ask Him for something just because you are His daughter and He loves to bless you.

NOTES

BEYOND COMFORT

BEYOND COMFORT

Devote yourselves to prayer, being watchful and thankful. And pray for us, too, that God may open a door for our message, so that we may proclaim the mystery of Christ, for which I am in chains. Pray that I may proclaim it clearly, as I should. Be wise in the way you act toward outsiders; make the most of every opportunity. Let your conversation be always full of grace, seasoned with salt, so that you may know how to answer everyone.

Colossians 4: 2-6

They say opportunity knocks but if it does, the times it has knocked in my life are few and far between. I have discovered that opportunity is something you make happen rather than waiting for it to come and find you. It doesn't arrive at your front door all packaged up with instructions of what it will involve and how to get started. It is more often discovered along the pathways of the purpose you are pursuing; you may find it at the road side of the journey you are already committed to taking. Many times we miss the very opportunities we are praying for because they don't arrive in the manner we had requested.

Often, the opportunity I have found does not create a sense of comfort, rather it comes with a very real cost and responsibility. Sometimes the opportunities we are supposed to embrace are waiting for us to go beyond what is usual and move into what will become for someone, or indeed for our own lives, a potential miracle. Opportunity likes to dress up and its preferred disguise is usually inconvenience. It hides amongst the errands we are avoiding and the conversation we are postponing, it is often found wearing the plain clothes called commitment and challenge. It's our ability to peer over the counter of comfort that then takes us into some beyond encounters that change our lives and the lives of those around us forever.

The opportunity to become an answer to another's need, to bring light to a dark place, the privilege of becoming someone's friend. The beyond moments to speak up, stand up and step up, not waiting for something to happen but instead, seizing the chance to make it happen. Colossians 4:5 is a huge challenge to all of our lives: "make the most of every opportunity". No matter how much we may feel we live this out, this verse suggests we need to look again, to aim not to miss a single moment. It asks us to test our hearts again, to challenge the weariness and commit afresh to going beyond comfort into the adventure that those moments create.

How often do we fail to see the opportunity or we see it but choose to ignore it because we believe our lives are already at capacity? Yet I have discovered that our capacity is linked to our level of willingness. We all have gifts and talents within our lives, God placed them there, so it's our job to unearth that potential and attach it to the ever unfolding purpose we are made to discover. Purpose lights dormant potential like a lightbulb that finds a lamp; when these two things come together everything changes.

CHAPTER SIX

What was hidden is now seen, what was an idea is now a reality, these two apart are brilliant inventions but together they find purpose and give light that benefits others. That's how opportunity works: when it finds willingness, it becomes the key that unlocks a new door and as the door opens so do new possibilities. Without willingness, generosity remains locked up, good ideas stay just ideas. Our decision to say yes, to volunteer, to show up, awakens not just what's in us but it can also unlock the world around us.

Living Beyond The Comfort Level

Have you ever decided to go and serve when you really felt you didn't have the time or space? Your willingness said yes. So when you were doing what you didn't think you wanted to do, you suddenly saw the beauty and blessing that opportunity became. New friendships were found, encouragement was given, you saw things differently. That decision to add willingness to your world has now become an appointment with new possibilities within your reach. Comfort will tell you to let it go but willingness will say, have a go.

Maybe you feel you have lived much of your life this way - being willing and being the one who says yes. If that's the case, well done and thank you for all the times your willingness has made a difference. For you the challenge is not so much in finding the willingness to help; you have seen its benefits first hand and have committed to keep stepping up wherever you can. Perhaps the beyond for you is that you have told yourself that what you do is all you can do and you have restricted your own level of encounter to where you think your skill set fits comfortably. You are living with the light on and you shine wherever you go but maybe the beyond God has for you is there in an increased capacity you have yet to discover. You have become so comfortable with what you do that you haven't asked, is that all I can do? Just as you can get different wattage in lightbulbs, maybe it's time to increase the wattage in your own life and see what lies beyond. God's best life for you is a life that removes the dimmer switch and takes away the lampshade that is stifling your brightness, whether that's your own doubts, the shade others bring or a lack of confidence you may have to break past where you have become settled, even stuck. So how bright does your life shine? Where is it time to say yes to a new opportunity and add more brightness by adding more willingness?

Living beyond the comfort level requires us to live with our eyes wide open and not just to what we have in front of us. It asks us to look at the need we would rather not see, feel the pain of our world, sooth the suffering and bring peace to the chaos. It asks us to not ignore what disturbs our hearts but instead say, I will allow my heart to be moved so that I can then get involved.

God will never put on you more than you can handle, yet He will invite you, as it says in Isaiah, to stretch your life and lengthen your reach. He will ask you to take the place where you do life and make it a place where expansion and increase can happen. So where is it time to stretch? Where have you started to say no and it should be a yes? What opportunity is on the roadside of your life and it's time for you to lengthen your reach and get involved? The opportunity to bless will never leave you feeling less, it will only increase your borders and become seeds sown for your future.

"

WILLINGNESS IS OFTEN THE WELCOME MAT FOR THE GUEST CALLED GREATNESS

BEYOND OPPORTUNITIES

When a Samaritan woman came to draw water, Jesus said to her, "Will you give Me a drink?" The Samaritan woman said to Him, "You are a Jew and I am a Samaritan woman. How can You ask me for a drink?" Jesus answered her, "If you knew the gift of God and who it is that asks you for a drink, you would have asked Him and He would have given you living water."

John 4:6-10

Galatians 5:25 says we are to "keep in step with the spirit", which means God wants us to allow Him to set the pace. When He is leading there is always an invitation to go beyond. His steps may at times seem like a detour but that's where we have to trust and follow. In this way we can learn how to live with a heart that is willing to be redirected so that an opportunity can be awakened. Jesus often stopped in unscheduled places and spent time with those on the margins of society. He had the greatest and most significant of assignments to achieve on earth but was always willing to extend His hand to those He saw along the way. He stopped for a woman at the well and transformed the simple act of drawing water into teaching her about the living water. That moment moved from getting a drink to a life forgiven and set free.

How many times do we pass by these scenarios in our everyday lives, when are we too busy to see woman at the well type of opportunities? Where do we rush past when we need to stay in step with the Spirit and pull up a seat for a moment? Jesus never allowed His schedule or what was easy or comfortable to get in the way of His acts of kindness. Jesus lived with His heart full of compassion, which made being uncomfortable normal. He felt others pain, He sensed their loss, He cried with those who grieved, He touched those who were unclean. Jesus lived way beyond any sense of comfort as His compassion caused Him to involve even when He wasn't asked. On another occasion Jesus was passing through a town and saw a funeral was taking place, His heart of compassion once more redirected His schedule. He saw an opportunity to help a woman who was burying her only son. She never once asked Jesus to intervene, she seemed unaware that He was even passing by yet Jesus didn't wait for an invitation, He simply stepped in and that day gave the woman her son back. He touched the coffin and His willingness led to a young man's resurrection.

There are so many examples of those whose lives were forever changed because Jesus chose to live in a way that was beyond comfort and convenience and instead chose to make every moment a potential miracle for someone. If every opportunity becomes a place of untapped possibility, then with that comes a demand for an increase of inconvenience and that is costly yet its rewards are way beyond what comfort could ever afford.

CHAPTER SIX

What if you could move your everyday living into the realm of beyond? Where your awareness of the people around you and the assignment in front of you became amplified. Where the ways you could help, speak up, love, include others, became magnified. What if you went from occasionally feeling you made a difference to a life that is daily on a collision course with purpose?

Jesus teaches us how to live beyond comfort in the story of the good Samaritan. Where opportunity lay at the side of the road, because it looked more like an inconvenience than a beneficial stop, others passed by. How often do we take the same approach? Passing by what seems too costly, demanding or distracting from what we want to do. Yet there was one in the story who didn't pass by but made the stranger a friend and the inconvenience a place of connection. He took what others saw as an obstruction and made it an opportunity to do good. Our lives are able to do just the same; we have to decide whether we cross the road so we can remain comfortable or step into others' stories so can become available. When Jesus was on His way to the next place he needed to be, He still lived His life ready to engage and help those who were along the way.

Often we are so focused on where we want to be, we fail to see where we are. We are so fascinated with getting to the next place, we fail to see the people in the current place. When we see our passing through places as opportunities waiting to be discovered, it changes everything. We begin to realise we are not waiting for an assignment, we are called to live on assignment. What impact do you have on the environment you are in? I passed through three years at university; that's where I lived and studied. It wasn't my permanent address, it was a passing place but while I was passing through I was surrounded by the opportunity to share my life, make new friends, bless other students, leave an impact for good in that community. There is power in the pass, not just in passing the final exam. I have lived in four different areas with my family, passing through four sets of neighbours and four communities. In each place, I had the power of the pass. I could make friends with new families, bless people on my street, know the names of the people in my area, make moments to engage and make a difference. We can either pass through on purpose or see these moments on the way to our destination, a distraction or even an inconvenience. What Jesus modelled and this scripture is asking, is for us to pass through on purpose and for purpose, making the power of the pass reach its full potential.

SHARE
YOUR BLESSING

When Jesus reached the spot, He looked up and said to him, "Zacchaeus, come down immediately. I must stay at your house today." So he came down at once and welcomed Him gladly. All the people saw this and began to mutter, "He has gone to be the guest of a sinner." But Zacchaeus stood up and said to the Lord, "Look, Lord! Here and now I give half of my possessions to the poor, and if I have cheated anybody out of anything, I will pay back four times the amount."

Luke 19:5-8

In Luke 19, Jesus was heading towards Jerusalem. He had the cross before Him and He was carrying a weight no one else could bear or ever understand. We are told in verse one that on His journey, "Jesus entered Jericho and was passing through" and once more, He made an unscheduled stop. Jesus passed through Jericho and as He did, He met a man whose life He changed forever: He put the keys of new life into the hands of Zacchaeus. In His passing through, He passed over not just forgiveness but acceptance and love. He invited himself to Zacchaeus house for dinner because He knew that to make the most of this opportunity, it wasn't enough to just speak a word. He needed to demonstrate His love by going to a home others would not enter and eating with a man considered a sinner and unworthy of such an honour.

Jesus wants to impact every life and then He wants all those His has impacted to pass that blessing on. When Jesus touches our lives, we should never keep that to ourselves. It's not a luxury for us to indulge in, a comfort to wrap around ourselves. We all have so much blessing to share. We have layer upon layer of wisdom, hope, truth and life to pass over. Where we do life everyday can become a place where we pass these things to others. Comfort would say, why bother? Beyond living says, let's make this go even further.

Did you ever play pass the parcel as a child? You pass along the present and when the music stops you get to take a layer off. There's a little treat between each layer so there is an opportunity for everyone to get something. That's how our lives are supposed to be lived. We are like that gift and we have layer upon layer of life to pass on. Each layer has something within it we may have received, learnt or heard and we now get to pass that over to others. The Spirit is like the DJ and wants to guide you when to pass the parcel and when to pause so someone can unwrap a layer.

The opportunities we are supposed to step into are the conversations and interactions that become a layer of life to someone else, enriching and encouraging them. If we don't tune into the Spirit, we will miss the many cues He wants to give us. When we rush past we fail to pass over what we have no right to hold onto any longer. We need the layers of generosity, kindness, love and acceptance to be passed along. They are the power in the pass that we get to make everyday.

The beautiful thing about how this works is, if we are willing to share our blessing, those who receive from us then get to pass it on to others. Zacchaeus wasn't the only one who the power of this pass would bless because he then went on to make the most of his moment too; he volunteered to pay back all those he had stolen from. He wanted to pass on the love and the forgiveness he had received and with his physical action, the power of the pass could continue.

So many others would now be blessed through Jesus choosing to spend a little time with a tax collector. Whatever we pass over, be it an act of kindness, time that we spend, love that we show, then creates the opportunity to keep being passed on. The recipient of your passing through could be changed forever and will then change the lives of others you might not even know about or ever encounter. Jesus had to leave that town, but because He passed through on purpose, though He wasn't going to remain there, the ripple effect of His time in Jericho could be seen long after He had left. That one moment was a lasting miracle of transformation that impacted a whole neighbourhood.

So what does this mean for our lives? If you live beyond comfort, you are asked to take every passing through place of your life and pass something along. Become aware of the opportunity all around you and be aware of the things that seek to stop and even blind you. When Jesus reached Zacchaeus and was passing over His words of acceptance, at that very moment the crowd got noisy, furious that Jesus had chosen this man to dine with, this sinner to spend time with. They began to try and block what was about to be blessed.

If you ever watch an NFL game, of which I have watched many, you will frequently hear the term 'pass interference'. It is an illegal play where the opposition is trying to stop the pass from happening. The enemy works in exactly the same way; he wants to create pass interference in all our lives. He doesn't want you and I to live beyond comfort, to share our blessings, because he knows that creates discomfort for him. He doesn't want us to disturb the norm or do more than what's usual. He places pass interference in our lives: things like apathy and familiarity. He works hard to let fear talk us out of stepping out; he wants us to doubt our ability and capacity so we restrict our willingness and avoid discovering the power of the pass.

We need to shout, just as they do in a game where this behaviour is happening, this is pass interference and it's an illegal move. The enemy has robbed too many moments through pass interference so determine again to live in a way that makes the most of every opportunity. Increase your willingness and decrease the interference. Share the blessing that is you with those that you come into contact with day by day. Live to make a difference because your life is just too precious and powerful to be contained in the armchair called comfort.

"

YOUR LIFE IS A GIFT AND ONLY YOU CAN GIVE IT AWAY

BEYOND
COMFORT

THE CHALLENGE

SEE IT

This month, identify four places that you regularly pass through: the place where you work; the neighbourhood you live in; the gym you use; your evening class; your kids' playground; the local petrol station; your regular grocery store. Choose just four, don't try to be an overachiever. Set yourself the challenge of how, in each of these areas, you can become someone who doesn't just pass by but you pass through on purpose. What can you do differently to make a difference? Some of the things you may have to consider will take you far outside your comfort zone but this month is a challenge to go beyond what is comfortable so even if it feels strange, be willing to have a go.

SAY IT

You are going to start some conversations this month with people God has placed in your world. These are opportunities you may have to work at to make them happen so write down some ways you are going to engage with those who you pass by everyday. Here's a few things you could try:

- In the place where you work, once a week take a packet of cookies in and make a point of leaving them in the staff room with a note to encourage your colleagues. Or have the treats on your desk and ask people to come over and grab a cookie and when they do start some new conversations.

- If that's something you find easy to do, take it a step beyond and this month choose certain people in your office to pray for everyday. Ask God to give you a word of encouragement for them and you will find He does. Be bold enough to go and just encourage the ones you feel led to do that for. Tell someone you are praying for them; no one is going to refuse prayer.

- In the neighbourhood where you live, pick up some extra groceries for an elderly neighbour, a new mum or someone who lives alone. Deliver your gift and perhaps as a family, invite your neighbours over.

DO IT

Go beyond what's comfortable and be willing to get involved. Take this challenge into your passing through places and start to be more deliberate this month about the pass. When you sense a pass interference, whether that's someone's negative response or a fear of what people might think, make sure you call it out as an illegal play. Don't let it shut you down. Journal the places you feel you are facing interference and decide to keep persisting with prayer and patience. This month track the new things you learn about those around you and commit to being someone who is more engaged in their lives so you can be more of an encourager to them.

NOTES

CHAPTER SEVEN

BEYOND REJECTION

BEYOND REJECTION

"Whatever town or village you enter, search there for some worthy person and stay at their house until you leave. As you enter the home, give it your greeting. If the home is deserving, let your peace rest on it; if it is not, let your peace return to you. If anyone will not welcome you or listen to your words, leave that home or town and shake the dust off your feet."

Matthew 10:11-14

How many times in life do we allow rejection to hijack our hearts and lives? Rejection is part of the landscape that we all must learn to navigate. I know we would rather skip over it or at all costs avoid it. However, when we begin to accept it is going to happen at times, then we can begin to move beyond where rejection would like to imprison us. We can start to see that actually there are times when the very thing that seems to be opposing us is the same thing God will use to grow us. We have to be able to see life beyond rejection or we will never go past the countertop of hurt and disappointment. We will never venture into what's beyond the cutting comment or the meanness of the moment and find the healing and purpose that awaits if we can get past this point. We have to commit, however difficult it may seem at times, to live a life that goes beyond the barrier that has blocked the way for too many believers: the barrier called rejection.

Maybe rejection for you has been a one off visitor but I know in my life it has tried one too many times to come and make itself a permanent house guest. No one gets to escape its visitation. Perhaps rejection came to your life early on as it does for so many, in the school classroom or playground. When the friend you thought was going to be forever turned out to be more fairweather. The group who had made you feel a sense of belonging now decided you didn't fit any more and revoked your membership. That rejection removed you for being on the inside to feeling like an outsider, sitting alone in the cafeteria, walking home by yourself. Rejection to one so young can be devastating. Its pain is profound in those formative years and you doubt you will ever find a friend again. To be honest, nothing much changes as we go from primary school to adulthood, those moments when it comes to friends can happen at any age and they hurt.

For some, rejection has been felt most in a failed marriage, for others it's your own family that seem to have made you sit on the outside and look in. Rejection can come with abuse and pain. The words of rejection sting like a poison; they enter your soul and slowly begin to contaminate your thinking and infringe your freedom and sense of belonging. Rejection says, you are not wanted, you have no purpose, it belittles your abilities and it uninvites you to the party. Rejection is cruel but God knew it was part of the life we would have to navigate. He left us with wisdom on how to deal with this menace so that when it seeks to sabotage our future, we would have an ability to move beyond.

CHAPTER SEVEN

Some of the best examples of those who took the rejection as a place of redirection are found in our family history, in the legacy we have been left by those who have gone before us in the faith. The stories of Joseph, Paul, David and Moses teach us that rejection can be the birthing place of finding something far greater that lies beyond. The life of Jesus is one of the best places we can go to to learn these lessons as He handled rejection in every area of His world. So for a moment, let's examine a few ways we can gain strength to move forward wherever we have allowed rejection to back us into a corner.

Assignment Rejection

Have you ever been rejected in a job situation? Maybe you didn't get the promotion or you were even demoted. Perhaps you applied for the job and were rejected in the interview. That happened to me when I was fresh out of university. Newly married and with a mortgage to pay, I needed a job. I had so many applications out but nothing was coming back and so, feeling desperate, I just looked for any work in the area. I remember going for an interview for the job as receptionist at a double glazing warehouse. I knew it wasn't what my degree was for but was sure I could just get this job while I waited to start my chosen career. Yep, you guessed it, the company rejected me. They told me I didn't have enough skills to run the reception. I remember leaving insulted, offended and mad. That rejection knocked my confidence and made me question my ability. That's what rejection does, it makes us doubt we have what it takes.

Jesus had rejection on His assignment; the religious leaders were constantly criticising His work. They would reject His methods and they would question His authority. Jesus would have rejection from those who were scholars and teachers and that rejection would keep pulling into question the validity of His assignment. However, Jesus used these points of rejection to not only affirm His assignment and reveal where His authority lay but He also used the rejection to rewrite the way that things had been done up until that point. He healed on a Sabbath, He touched the lepers, He preached to the women and He blurred the lines between class and culture. Jesus used the points of rejection as places for expansion.

We also need to allow the place where we feel our assignment is rejected to be the place we move beyond. My job rejection caused me to go beyond the voices of criticism and instead become even more committed to making a difference. I still drive past that window company every now and then and when I do I say, thank you for rejecting me as underqualified because it caused me to go beyond and pursue my purpose without needing everyone's permission. Jesus told His disciples in Matthew 10, when you come to a place and you find people slam the door in your face, when they reject the assignment you are on, don't get upset, don't quit, just shake the dust off your feet and move on. The assignment is too important to allow someone's personal preference to prevent what is in you coming out of you. The way to live beyond rejection is to regularly practice shaking the dust off.

"

REJECTION MAY BE YOUR OPPORTUNITY FOR REDIRECTION

RELATIONAL REJECTION

Jesus went to Nazareth, where He had been brought up, and on the Sabbath day He went into the synagogue, as was His custom. He stood up to read, and ... He found the place where it is written:

"The Spirit of the Lord is on me,
because He has anointed me
to proclaim good news to the poor..."

The eyes of everyone in the synagogue were fastened on Him. He began by saying to them, "Today this scripture is fulfilled in your hearing." All the people in the synagogue were furious when they heard this. They got up, drove Him out of the town, and took Him to the brow of the hill on which the town was built, in order to throw Him off the cliff. But He walked right through the crowd and went on His way.

Luke 4:16-30

I'm sure you have heard the term friendly fire: it's when in a time of war someone is injured or killed by a bullet that came from someone on the same side. In the chaos someone becomes a casualty of one who was supposed to be a friend. Friendly fire happens all the time in our lives, in fact it's more often the stray bullet from someone close that does more damage than the attack from the stranger. If we have no awareness that this is possible and even more it is probable, then we will be taken out at first hit. The enemy will always look for those who are close enough to take a shot at your life, as those with a better proximity have more likelihood of making sure they hit the target.

There have been times in my life when the pain of relational rejection has almost caused me to quit. No-one is free from the pain of relational breakdown and that's why we need to know the rejection doesn't mean we resign from our call, commitment and passion. The more you say yes to leading, the more you have to navigate relational rejection. I recall an incident in my life that almost took me out. The rejection came from someone I was so close to and it hurt in a way that only those who you trust the most can ever inflict. What had been a beautiful friendship for many years began to become sour. Jealousy and pride took centre stage and where before words of encouragement had been spoken, now words of criticism and unkindness were more common. Yet despite many attempts to rebuild, the relationship moved to a point that was beyond repair. The friend chose to walk away, not just from our friendship but also from everything they had said they held dear. The sadness in these moments can be so strong as you grieve the loss of something you placed such value on. It can affect your entire family, team and community and you can't help but take it personally and question where you went wrong. The truth is, often the reasons are way beyond our control but what we pick up in the pile of debris left behind is offense and bitterness, making it harder to trust anyone else or build relationally in the future. The enemy wants you to not just feel rejected but also to feel a sense of failure and resentment. He is not just wanting to shut you down emotionally but also cause you to lose perspective and cause the place of rejection to become your place of resignation.

Jesus, in the first stages of His ministry, was about to discover that those who knew Him best were not going to be the ones who would encourage Him in taking His next step. When He came to Nazareth, He did not hear cheers of encouragement but rather found words of rejection and judgement.

CHAPTER SEVEN

In this place, Jesus had friends he had grown up with, aunts and uncles that had taken care of Him, a whole town he had worked and interacted with. So when He went there, aware of the ministry and mission He was to carry, He wanted to go and bless those who He had shared so much of His life with. I am sure as He entered Nazareth, He knew the ones who needed a miracle, the neighbour that had been long term sick, the ones who were in pain and needed to find hope again. Jesus had entered Nazareth to bless and yet what He found from those He loved was rejection. They couldn't accept the change that had taken place in Jesus; they wouldn't acknowledge the mission on His life and the words of rejection reduced Jesus from Son of God to just Joseph's boy.

Jesus was unable to be Himself any more in the place that had been such a huge part of His journey. He couldn't bless where He had been blessed, He couldn't help those who had helped Him, not because He didn't want to but because they didn't want Him to. Sometimes we have to endure the friendly fire of rejection that comes from our own families, those whom we have lived so much of our life with. Remember Joseph whose own brothers rejected him through jealousy and envy? Joseph, who did not ask for the coat or the dreams, was rejected because of his brothers' insecurity. The same happened for David, whose brothers saw no potential in him and whose father didn't even invite him to the anointing party in 1 Samuel 16.

This rejection that comes from such close proximity is dangerous and if we don't learn to identify and deal with it, we could end up quitting, drowning in the pit or not showing up for our own destiny party. So how do you get beyond this rejection? You do what Jesus, Joseph and David did, you keep moving. You don't waste time trying to prove you should be accepted. You don't try and argue with the ones who never want to be convinced there is another possibility. Jesus moved on from Nazareth, Joseph built a life beyond the pit and David showed up for the party and let God's presence speak for itself. Rejection became redirection, it didn't become resignation. It doesn't mean it isn't painful or disappointing when family and loved ones shut you out; it hurts like few other things can. It is the last place you should be and that's why it's the last place you should stay. We can't look to people for what only God himself can give. There is a life beyond this friendly fire, you will heal and you may even find restoration, as Joseph did with his family but when he was reunited, he was no longer looking for acceptance: he had found a life beyond that and so must you.

REBELLIOUS REJECTION

Wanting to release Jesus, Pilate appealed to them again. But they kept shouting, "Crucify Him! Crucify Him!" For the third time he spoke to them: "Why? What crime has this man committed? I have found in Him no grounds for the death penalty. Therefore I will have Him punished and then release Him." But with loud shouts they insistently demanded that He be crucified, and their shouts prevailed.

Luke 23: 20-23

If you're a parent, you won't find this type of rejection hard to understand. If you have ever had the child you love and care for go against what you are saying, you will have had to deal with rebellious rejection. This kind of rejection is usually nothing to do with you but it feels so undeserved as it manifests in words and actions that are so ungrateful for all you have done. Like the prodigal whose rebellion saw him leave home and squander all his father had worked to provide for him, these moments can become a rejection that makes you want to withhold and refrain from blessing one more person. Jesus endured this kind of rebellious rejection. It was most manifest when He was about to go to the cross, in that moment that Pontius Pilate asked the crowd who they should save that day. Jesus stood before all the faces who He had ministered to; people in that crowd He had healed, families He had restored, lives He had blessed and brought purpose to. In their rebellious riotous mood they shouted, crucify Him. That rebellious rejection sent Jesus to the cross and saw a murderer released.

Moses had to deal with a rebellious rejection. After leading millions from captivity to freedom, he found that they began to rebel and grumble and complain against the servant of God, who had risked his own life going to speak to Pharaoh so they could be liberated. Moses, who had led the people out of obedience to God, was now surrounded by the groans and moans of the same people who felt that he had not done enough. He was so mad at the ungratefulness of the children of Israel he lost his temper. We may also feel just like Moses. We may feel, why should I have to deal with this kind of rejection? Why lead people who are rejecting me, why serve those who don't appreciate me, why should I rescue those who are rebelling against me? Well, just like the picture of God in the story of the prodigal, we are called to go beyond the rebellious rejection and show outrageous acceptance. The prodigal didn't deserve the acceptance from the home he rejected but that's the point. A beyond understanding uses the place of rejection for the breaking of ground called acceptance. Jesus was hung on the cross by a rebellious crowd who rejected him but on that cross He went beyond and broke open the grave so everyone could find acceptance through Him, as we read in Luke 23:24 when Jesus said: "Father, forgive them, for they do not know what they are doing".

CHAPTER SEVEN

So where does this challenge meet your life? What area do you need to allow healing to flow so that you can move beyond rejection? Going back to where we began, every parent knows that when the toddler is having a tantrum and shouting at you to go away, you don't leave the house or ask the toddler to leave home. You go beyond because you know this is rebellion speaking. This is anger and frustration being given the microphone and the only way to change the conversation is not by adding more rejection to the rebellion but by acceptance. It's the willingness for the parent to ride out the tantrum that eventually leads to the child giving up and asking for that hug. If your teenager is rebelling and in doing so you are the one they are rejecting, don't take it so personally that you lose your perspective. I am sure when Jesus saw the ones He had loved shouting 'crucify Him', He had to choose to either see the crowd through the eyes of resentment or see them through the eyes of restoration. Don't allow rebellious rejection to become a personal statement. It's not about you, it's often about what they are going through. Therefore the decision has to be, are you willing to go beyond and wait for them to get through this rejection, so you can be there for them at the exit with arms open in acceptance?

Rejection can become a powerful thing when we learn to take the poison out of its sting. Rejection can lead to a place that's beyond the moment and introduce you to a way of living that is able to use rejection for redirection where necessary. Rejection can become the place where you rewrite the rules and it can even become the place where you learn new skills. Beyond rejection is a much deeper level of acceptance, not just of others but also of ourselves. Jesus was rejected and He warned his disciples in John 15, "If they persecuted Me, they will persecute you also". He warned them because He wanted then to learn now how to move beyond later.

We are Christ's disciples and we carry the same message of good news. Don't be surprised if the people that are closest to you sometimes reject what God is doing in and through you - the message you carry and the mission you are assigned. What happened in the playground at school can also happen on the playing fields of life. Just as you can look back now and see those moments don't define you or derail you, you need to remind yourself neither will the moments you are facing now or will face in the future. Rejection won't define you but if you learn to live beyond, it may instead beautifully refine you.

BEYOND
REJECTION

THE CHALLENGE

SEE IT

This month, rejection can become your redirection. If you accept this challenge, in the place where you feel you have been imprisoned by rejection, where it has stolen your voice or your confidence, you can begin to channel your energy in a different direction. Identify the place where you feel rejected and the people you feel have rejected you. Instead of ignoring it, see that area and be bold enough to write it down: this will become your prayer list for the month. What's your equivalent of that pit moment for Joseph - the place where you feel your worth, your ideas, your contribution is rejected, where you doubt you have anything to offer? Where have you allowed a failure or a misunderstanding to lock you down? Joseph in his rejection didn't try to prove his innocence and worth, he just got on with growing his life. Right now use the rejection to redirect you. Take the no to the job you applied for as the yes for you to go after something different; the no to the relationship as a direction to look for new places of connection. Start to redraw the map of your life, picture the possibilities in your future - if you can see it, then you can begin to plan it.

SAY IT

The challenge now is to pray over those places and people associated with your rejection a blessing; to not allow how they made you feel to become how you treat others. Challenge yourself to not give anymore airtime to the pain and instead redirect your energy into purpose. You can't move beyond unless you deal with what you are facing now so challenge yourself to get out of the pit; begin to change your confession and choices now so you can start to climb out of where you have been stuck. Next to the places and names you have written, write the ways you are going to challenge yourself to move on. Pick yourself up and dust yourself off.

_____
_____
_____
_____
_____
_____
_____
_____
_____
_____
_____
_____
_____
_____
_____
_____
_____
_____
_____
_____
_____
_____
_____
_____
_____
_____

DO IT

Finally, challenge yourself this month to channel all the rejection from the past into a commitment to building the palace of your future. Imagine a different possibility. Instead of seeing no worth, see the possibility of changing people's lives way beyond those borders. Challenge yourself to get palace ready like Joseph; he was in the prison but his plans were for the palace. Don't wait until the circumstances change, you can make the changes now. You need to lift your thinking and start planning again. Instead of focusing on what you have lost, redirect your energy into what is to come. This month make a list of things you need to do to make the rejection a redirection. What application do you need to fill in, appointment do you need to make, conversation do you need to initiate? Start somewhere and you will find by the end of the month, you have moved forward from the place where you were previously stuck.

NOTES

CHAPTER EIGHT

BEYOND
WORTHY

BEYOND
WORTHY

"'Holy, holy, holy is the Lord God Almighty, who was, and is, and is to come." Whenever the living creatures give glory, honour and thanks to Him who sits on the throne and who lives for ever and ever, the twenty-four elders fall down before Him who sits on the throne and worship Him who lives for ever and ever. They lay their crowns before the throne and say: "You are worthy, our Lord and God, to receive glory and honour and power."

Revelation 4:8-11

Recently, on a trip to London, I had the privilege of going with my family for a tour around the House of Lords in the Palace of Westminster. I love history and was excited about showing our children some of the great traditions and values our nation had been built upon. As we walked around this incredible building we were made aware of the legacy that had been passed down over generations, paintings and statues of leaders that had helped bring reformation in our nation. The more we saw, the more I became aware of just how much etiquette and protocol was involved in our history, the respect for title and position. The House of Commons and House of Lords were separated out by social class, with traditional expectations of how things must be done, even different coloured carpets for the different social groups to walk upon. No matter what your view of the monarchy or this hierarchical system, one thing is for sure: with the crown there also comes a demand for a change in behaviour. You wouldn't just go up to royalty and say hello; there is a way of greeting royalty that people adhere to, even to this day. If royalty entered your front room right now, your behaviour would change but the incredible reality is, we have an audience with royalty all the time.

We serve the Lord of heaven and earth. His title is unrivaled, His majesty is greater than any monarchy has ever seen. I have to ask myself the question, do I show the correct honour and respect in my response to being in the presence of such greatness? Have I become careless and almost flippant with His presence? Have I forgotten that He is the King of kings and Lord of lords, that the crown on His head was the crown that gave me access to a life after death? The Majesty of heaven, the Lamb who was slain, the Lion of Judah, Almighty God presences Himself with us here on earth. This concept seems so outrageous to our natural minds and hard to fathom in our daily routines of life. It is easy for us to become familiar with something so spectacular. We are all guilty at times of overlooking this great privilege that presents itself to each of us. Have we lost the awe and wonder? Have we forgotten to bow our knee in His presence and to humble ourselves in reverence? Perhaps we need to look again at how we see the King of kings and take our worship and devotion, giving and serving, beyond.

CHAPTER EIGHT

In Revelation we are told that in heaven, the angels continually bow down saying holy holy. It speaks of God being the only one worthy of such honour and praise. Yet in our modern and changing world, maybe we have allowed our best praise to be misdirected and our worship to become diluted. What if we could change that? What if we could start to bring back that sense of awe and wonder into our everyday lives? What if we were to start to act differently because we are aware more than ever before that we are in the presence of the King?

Beyond Worship

How many times have you been at a worship service and found yourself distracted or disconnected? You have sung along and may even have lifted a hand in response but you were going through the motions, not actually adoring God and giving Him your worship as an offering. This can happen for many reasons and when it does we must be careful not to arrive at the wrong conclusion for though you may feel a sense of disconnection in that moment, it is still no less full of His presence. The King of kings is in the room whether you feel it or not. Our disconnection does not equal distance, it is more a symptom of our own detachment and lack of awareness.

When we reduce worship to singing a few songs, we remove from our life something not only powerful but so very beautiful. Worship is one of the very few things you can give to God. Your sacrifice of praise, your songs of adoration and proclamation are your gifts back to God to tell Him of your love and to express to Him your gratitude. Worship is a vehicle that allows you to honour your Creator and magnify His name over every other name. Discovering the power of worship will take your love and commitment beyond singing in a service into a daily discipline and devotion. The ability to at any time bow your knee or lift your voice to sing out your gratitude should never be contained to a time and space once a week; it's something we need to move to a realm beyond. It might be acceptable to say, I love you, to those closest to you once a year or even once a month but it doesn't mean that it is enough. The words of love and affirmation should not be held back for a special occasion; everyday is an opportunity to mention your love and gratitude for those you cherish in your world.

Worship is your, I love you, moment to Jesus, it's the way you create a place of intimacy with the King in the middle of all the other demands of your day. Worship removes you from the routine even if it's just for a few moments and it places you in the room with royalty. Worship makes you more aware of His presence than your own. Worship reminds you of how worthy He is and how much praise He deserves. When we start to move our worship beyond we find our whole world begins to change.

The atmosphere changes in our home, car, workplace. You don't need the church worship band in your front room, worship is about you adoring your King. In Psalm 22 we are told that God sits enthroned on the praises of His people. God wants to inhabit your praise so wherever you are, you can build a place for God's presence. Invite God to be enthroned on your songs of worship. The thought that God Almighty wants to come and inhabit our world is mind blowing. It is an honour and a privilege beyond any of our comprehension. Let's not neglect something so very powerful that we have been given unlimited access to.

CHAPTER EIGHT

"

THE KING OF KINGS IS PRESENT AND YOU HAVE HIS FULL ATTENTION

BEYOND
ADORATION

For the word of God is alive and active.
Sharper than any double-edged sword,
it penetrates even to dividing soul and
spirit, joints and marrow; it judges the
thoughts and attitudes of the heart.

Hebrews 4:12

We can become all too familiar at times with the way we see and approach God. While we should never feel afraid to come before Him, we should also never lose sight of who we are approaching. That way our worship won't become watered down or even wasteful and our time in His presence will become something we see as precious and powerful.

Perhaps you have worship music on all the time but it's become so familiar, it's more background noise than a deliberate choice. I think worship can become like that, when we sing the songs over and over there can be a sense of disconnection. However, if the angels are singing on repeat holy holy and mean those words everytime, then the repetition is not the issue. It's our recognition of His holiness that is the hindrance; we have forgotten how holy He is, how worthy He is, we are singing to God as if we are just singing along to the radio. Surely we need at times to remind ourselves whose presence we are in and that we have an audience with the King.

We can make our worship about lyrics and cool musical arrangements more than simply adoration and connection. Some of the best worship is when you write your own lyrics as you just pour out your praise. The greatest songs are not the ones with the most downloads but the ones you upload from the depths of your soul. Worship isn't an industry or a performance, it's an opportunity for intimacy in His presence. So where is your worship in need of going beyond? Where have you got stuck and lost that sense of wonder? Allow your heart time to worship. Focus on the One who is worthy. Think on His majesty. When Moses was in the presence of God in Exodus 3, he removed his shoes for he realised he was standing on holy ground. We too stand on that same holy ground. What a thought for our hearts to ponder; what a truth for us to discover.

Beyond Devoted

The same scenario can be true when it comes to our attitude towards the word of God. We can see the Bible as a historical guide book or we can see it as words that can change our lives today. We can listen to messages preached as information or we can see them as places where God's word for our lives is imparted. The word of God is living and active and in order for our lives to move beyond where they currently are, we need revelation over information. The word of God is your invitation to go beyond with God. It is a place for you to seek wisdom and discover truth. It is light to your path and freedom for your future.

It is strength and correction. The word is there for you to venture beyond. Many people never leave the shallow end when it comes to their devotion, they feel unqualified to dive into the word thinking they need a degree to get anything from their scripture readings but the Bible is your life manual. The Spirit of God wants to help you find the truth of God's word so you can apply it to your heart and mind.

Remember when you were learning to read? At first you were so confused and frustrated, wondering if all these letters would ever make sense. The only way you overcame that obstacle was by committing to continuing to try to read the words on the page, to let the teacher guide you. The more times you applied yourself, the easier it became until eventually, what had been a mystery became words that created stories, inviting you on adventure and giving you a whole new world to discover. Taking your devotional life beyond is exactly the same: you have to learn to read all over again. Learn how to hear God's voice within the pages of the Old and New Testament. Learn wisdom that applies in your situation right now.

How do you start? You start with a renewed determination to go deeper. You pray and ask God to guide you. You can get devotional studies that can help you along the way and you read a little more everyday. You look at scripture and you start to see the truth that wants to become your truth. Don't hold it off any longer, move your love and devotion to His word beyond a sermon you amen on Sunday to a daily commitment to open the pages of your Bible and ask God to speak to your heart; I have a feeling He will do just that.

I fell in love with the word of God when I was 14. I remember God using the life of Timothy to help me understand how important this discipline was. When Paul is teaching his young student about spiritual authority and equipping him for ministry, he instructs Timothy to devote himself to scripture, to reading of the word. Paul was letting Timothy know, if you want to be used widely by God, then you need to go deeper with God. The words Timothy would later speak had to first be the ones he studied and understood. We need a fresh commitment to go beyond in our devotions. We can help more people find truth and understand their purpose when we ourselves have taken the time to unpack more of the scriptures. If we want the word to be living and active we need to first commit to being alert and connected in our own times of devotion.

I remember when I was at school seeing students who would learn the bare minimum for a test and just hope no questions would come up in the topics they hadn't bothered to study. When we live with just sound bites of truth, we are like those students, we hope we know enough to get us by but when the question we weren't expecting is asked, or we find ourselves in a place we didn't foresee and need wisdom to navigate, then we realise that having just enough is not good enough. Take your learning, understanding and devotion beyond what you think you should know to a place where you learn how to love discovering more about God and His word. There is so much more for you, so many more things God wants to speak to you. They are just waiting for you to access them by committing to be more devoted to the discipline of understanding who God is, for it is in our knowledge of Him we see a greater revelation of whom we are called to be. So many of our beyond answers rest in our willingness to become better students.

"

THE MORE WE EXERCISE THE POWER OF PRAYER, THE STRONGER A WEAPON IT BECOMES IN OUR LIFE

BEYOND
PRAYER

_____

For we do not have a high priest who is unable to empathise with our weaknesses, but we have One who has been tempted in every way, just as we are - yet He did not sin. Let us then approach God's throne of grace with confidence, so that we may receive mercy and find grace to help us in our time of need.

Hebrews 4:15-16

When we live with a sense of awe and wonder of who God is, it leads us to want to worship beyond and to be devoted to learning more about Him. This adoration will also shift our prayer life into a whole new gear. If prayer is your conversation with God, then why wouldn't you make the very most of that access that you have been given? You have an audience with the King and we are told to come boldly before the throne of God. He has invited you and I to come into His presence not to just worship but also to ask and seek of Him. Prayer is so powerful and like a muscle, the more we exercise the power of prayer, the stronger a weapon it becomes in our life.

The Bible tells us in James 5:16 that the prayers of a righteous man are effective, so why have we at times made prayer the emergency life raft only for use in times of need? Prayer is our everyday conversation with God. We can pray when we walk, while we are working, when we're out and about running errands. Prayer should be as natural as breathing. We have the ear of the King, why would we not want to speak and share with Him the things that are on our hearts? We are encouraged to pray throughout scripture and even given a template for how to pray with the Lord's prayer in Matthew 6. As we discovered in going beyond in our ask in chapter five, we are all invited to move into something for more intimate, the type of prayer life that moves us beyond presenting a list of needs to God. We have the possibility of moving into a relationship where through prayer, we not only talk to God but exchange and encounter His power in our lives and the lives of those that we are bringing before Him.

When was the last time you prayed out loud? When did you last take that power of prayer and pray for someone in your world? When did you last pray against spiritual darkness and fight with the weapon of prayer for freedom? Prayer is deeply personal but it is also incredibly powerful. It can be quiet but it can also be loud and fierce. Prayer can be a declaration of confidence in the presence of the One who holds the answers, an assertion of the authority that is found in His name over every other name.

In Matthew 17, we are told that the disciples came across a young boy possessed by a demon. They tried to deliver him from his torment but were unable to do so. Jesus rebuked the disciples for not understanding the authority that was theirs to take a hold of against this demonic attack.

CHAPTER EIGHT

The had not realised that their faith, even if it was as small as mustard seed, could move this mountain. Jesus cast out the boy's demons and silenced the darkness. He prayed with an understanding of the power of His conversation with the Father and if we want a beyond relationship with God, we also must learn the power of our conversation with Him.

The beyond prayer life doesn't stop when it's hard, it doesn't only pray in times of need. The beyond prayer life is consistent and persistent, it is asking, seeking and knocking until an answer is found. A beyond prayer life expects an answer and keeps trusting during the delays. It keeps praying with thanksgiving even when the answer seems to be tarrying. Sometimes we stop praying because we allow disappointment to edit our conversation with God but we need to move our prayer beyond this temporary expectation to an eternal revelation. Why only give God limited options in how He should respond? He has much greater plans than we can even imagine when we leave our lives in His hands. Move your prayer life into a conversation that believes, trusts and knows that God is in control. Pray with faith, with strength and with authority for it's in His name you are praying and His name is over everything.

What would happen if we each moved our life into this expression of beyond? How would our worship change, our understanding grow and our prayers become more effective? When did we forget we are in the presence of the King and where did we lose our sense of awe and wonder? Once we capture even just a small measure of how worthy and holy He is, our worship will find new words, our song will become stronger. When we magnify His vastness and His all knowing all powerful presence, we will hunger for more of His word and thirst for greater revelation of whose we are. We will stand to attention in our hearts and bow our knees in reverence. We will not waste our audience with the King on trivia or by giving Him leftovers. We will bring our best worship and pray such certain prayers for we know the One we are conversing with is not man that he could fail us but the living God who created us. He is beyond worthy of our honour, beyond worthy of our praise, beyond worthy of our attention and affection.

BEYOND
WORTHY

THE CHALLENGE

SEE IT

This month, it's time to move beyond in our devotional disciplines. Let's invite the presence of God to overwhelm and overtake in a way that moves our understanding, asking, seeing and praising to another level.

I lift up my eyes to you, to you who sit enthroned in heaven. Psalm 123.1

God wants to open your eyes and show you revelation for your own journey. He wants to show you how His word is alive and active so this month, it's time not just to read the word but to take the time to see the living and active word of God. Pray for your eyes to be opened afresh, ask for new insight as you read, ask God to show you His heart for people and the world around you. Can you see him in all His majesty? Can you linger in His presence longer and see more of who He is and therefore who you are? Where do you need to open your eyes and look at the Creator and all the beauty of creation? Make a commitment to press refresh in your devotional life so you see and hear things differently.

SAY IT

"For where two or three gather in my name, there am I with them." Matthew 18.20

What can you do to move your study time and your prayer life to new levels? Perhaps your devotional prayer time is private so a challenge would be to step out and pray with others, as we are called to do in Matthew 18. Take some time to examine how you pray and look at the ways you can go beyond. Commit to moving your time of devotion forward by adding new disciplines that will ask you to go deeper, making your devotional life bolder and more powerful. Write out a list of things you want to understand more and use this to focus your faith and your study so you can deepen your devotions.

DO IT

David was dancing before the Lord with all his might. Samuel 6.14

Where is your devotion stuck? Has it become attached to a service on a weekend? Do you pigeonhole your time with God into a short, set slot? Where can you move your praise, your prayer, your study into a new realm? Can you bring worship into your home life or your workplace? Can you discipline yourself to make your time with your Maker your absolute priority? Do it for this month. You'll be amazed how quickly the habit forms and it will be the best habit you ever make. David danced before the Lord will all his might. He took his worship beyond in an outward action so where can you do the same? Add some more actions to your devotions this month and see the difference it makes.

NOTES

CHAPTER NINE

BEYOND
AWARE

BEYOND AWARE

"Enter through the narrow gate. For wide is the gate and broad is the road that leads to destruction, and many enter through it. But small is the gate and narrow the road that leads to life, and only a few find it. Watch out for false prophets. They come to you in sheep's clothing, but inwardly they are ferocious wolves."

Matthew 7:13-15

Recently a strange situation happened that got me thinking. It was a cold dark evening and I had been shopping with my friend in the great city of Leeds. On our way home, I remembered we needed a few groceries and said I would quickly drop into the store we were passing. My friend decided to wait outside with all our shopping bags. As I was inside scanning my few items, a lady entered the store and rather abruptly demanded money back from items that had clearly just been stolen from the aisles. Her aggressive nature was clearly intimidating the young boy behind the checkout who looked like it was his first day on the job, so I tried to help him out and eventually the lady, realising she was not going to get any money, left the store shouting abuse. As I was telling my friend what had taken place, she realised that the same lady had asked her to watch her dog while she went in the store. In effect my friend had unwittingly been her accomplice; she was watching the dog and so enabling the chaos to happen.

We did find it quite funny but later that evening, I began to think a little more about how often this can happen and how the results of these scenarios are definitely not funny. How often does our inability to discern things make us enablers of the wrong things? How many times have we done the equivalent of watching the dog while someone's poor choice plays out? We can't prevent the wrong choices or the bad behaviour from happening but maybe we can become more aware that the wrong response makes us an enabler. Our lives need more awareness of not just what's happening around us but also what we are giving our voice and strength to.

Not every task needs your yes, not every opportunity needs you to take it and not every invitation means you should attend. We need to move beyond the craving to be needed or the drive to be popular. We need to be able to discern the right response in each opportunity that presents itself. Jesus told the disciples all the time to be discerning, to be not just awake but beyond that, to be aware. The Bible tells us the thief comes to steal, kill and destroy. He is not coming to mess around, he is coming to seriously mess things up.

Often it is our lack of awareness that can lead us to being more careless with the things around us. We fail to live with a sense of alert in the absence of an obvious attack. We have all done it, left the house without setting the alarm, left the keys by the door saying no-one will ever break in. We leave the door wide open for an enemy to come in when we live spiritually unaware. Matthew 7 warns us to look out for those who are like a wolf in sheep's clothing, those who enter the fold only to disrupt and destroy. It speaks about catching those little foxes that ruin the vine in Song of Solomon 2:15. The word of God is saying, in all your loving, trusting, reaching and building, add some security, be aware. In all the ways you are blessing and extending grace, don't overlook the need to also be wise.

Watch The Dog

So what are some of the dogs we need to stop watching? Proverbs 26:17 tells us that involving in someone else's quarrel is like grabbing a dog by the ears. This is great wisdom: maybe your life right now is filled with a lot of drama and the way to lessen that drama is to start removing yourself from certain situations. If my children have a disagreement, inevitably one of them may come to me and tell me their side of the story and ask me to go and sort things out. While I want peace and want to bring resolve, I have had to realise this argument isn't mine and therefore its resolution does not rest with me. They will never grow if I keep being the referee.

Solomon was put in the position of adjudicator in I Kings 3. Two women were arguing over whose baby was still alive but Solomon refused to take sides and simply said, let's cut the living baby in half and give each woman a part of the child. This decision shocked everyone in the room and yet it was the very way they found resolution. His wisdom was based on his beyond awareness that this argument could not be settled with negotiation. Instead it needed someone to say, I am not going to stand by and enable this deceit, I am going to make a decision that will move us beyond the confusion into resolution. Like Solomon, we need wisdom to know how to deal with the dysfunction and navigate the hostility, not complicate the problem. We need to discern more and enable less. Discernment requires us to not react but to lean into that still small voice, the whisper of awareness that is often drowned out by the noise of the things competing for your attention. Sometimes your proximity to a person can be the very thing that they use to enable a poor decision, using your presence as approval when in reality you thought you were just 'watching the dog'. Where are you holding something you need to put down, facilitating drama that needs no more actors?

We can get supporting and enabling mixed up; they sound similar but are actually very different. One is helpful and the other is most definitely harmful. We feel bad if we say, I can't help, while knowing it doesn't do the right kind of good when we do help. Beyond awareness is the ability to discern when your words are necessary and when they are not. When your intervention is a good deed and where it is just adding interference. Enabling actions maintain the status quo, they don't demand change or confront the problem. Lending the money that is adding to the poor financial choices is watching the dog. Keeping the secret so the behaviour can remain unchallenged. Not talking about the addiction is enabling the worst outcome. Beyond awareness is being willing to be bold enough to change things for the better. We need to have an awareness of what it takes to go beyond what people want, to attain what they actually need. They may want you to watch the dog but what they may need is for you to say, no more, I can't watch this dog, it's not helpful and then excuse yourself and walk away before you become the accomplice to another poor choice.

CHAPTER NINE

"

WHEN OUR CORNERSTONE IS CHRIST, EVERY OTHER ADDITION FINDS ITS RIGHT ALIGNMENT

ROCK OR SAND?

"If you work these words into your life,
you are like a smart carpenter who built
his house on solid rock. Rain poured
down, the river flooded, a tornado hit—
but nothing moved that house. It was
fixed to the rock. But if you just use My
words in Bible studies and don't work
them into your life, you are like a stupid
carpenter who built his house on the
sandy beach. When a storm rolled in
and the waves came up, it collapsed like
a house of cards."

Matthew 7:24-27 (MSG)

We need beyond awareness when it comes to what we are building our lives upon. The parable of the house on the rock tells us that there were two types of builders and both built impressive structures. From the outside they both looked substantial and credible. The difference, however, was in their foundations. The awareness of what they were built upon changed the outcome drastically. Often we are so impressed by what we see, we believe those visible results are the proof that this is a life, ministry, relationship that is well built. Yet the truth is, we have to move beyond being impressed by things we perceive and be willing to deepen our awareness when it comes to actually seeing things from the foundation up. Too many times we have given our approval to buildings that over time come crumbling down because all along they were on the sand and not the rock.

We need an awareness of where the fault lines are when it comes to the things we build. In San Andreas, California, there is a massive fault line that runs under the surface of the earth, invisible to the human eye. People bought homes and invested in buildings that were built in that part of the world. However, if they had made themselves more aware of the ground they were building on, if they had done more research into the geology, they would have found out the dangers of the fault line that lay beneath. The fault was always there and its menacing ability to undo any building if it was disturbed was always a possibility. Of course, if you choose to, you can still build on a fault line but you must have an awareness that it exists so that the building can be constructed of the right materials.

Spiritually, we can have fault lines in parts of our world; we can have a relationship we are committed to but we also know has fault lines through it. Knowing where and how deep the fault line lays means we build with more wisdom and accommodate the potential weakness by adding more strength. Ignorance builds anywhere with anyone and anything but it is wisdom that looks for the rock on which it can build. Maybe you need to do some surveys for your future: survey the land and write the report. The information is not there to put you off but rather it acts like an insurance policy, helping protect and better cover you for what's ahead.

Remember in Numbers 13 when the spies went into Canaan to see the lay of the land? They were going so they could increase their awareness of what they had to work with. They were going to see where they needed to add strength so they could build well. However, the report came back negative and instead of allowing the trip to be an information gathering exercise to give them greater awareness, the expedition ended in doubt and negativity, concluding it would be a disaster. Yet the report never needed to shut down their mission, rather it was essential information to improve their awareness of what they would need to make this miracle happen. Awareness is about taking the facts and then adding faith. It's not avoiding the work; it's forward planning for what's required. We need more wise master builders who are aware of the land, the soil, the materials. Builders who know how to deal with the fault line, and who aren't afraid to see the potential for both good and bad because this informs how they will build.

We need a beyond wisdom that doesn't settle for sand when it can find the rock. The more we are aware the better we can prepare. In Luke 14:13 it tells us that a king will count his troops before going to war. You wouldn't start a building project without first working out the costs. It's foolish to begin what you cannot afford to complete; ignorance of the costs will lead to failure of the whole project. We need to not be frightened to move our awareness beyond. See the cost so you know what you need to add to your account. See where the sand is so you don't build on what is temporary but instead, you build where it will make a lasting difference.

The Bible repeatedly describes Christ as our cornerstone (see Zechariah 10:4, Acts 4:11, Ephesians 2:20 and others). The cornerstone is a term builders use for the first brick that they lay when they are building. That becomes the anchor and alignment for every other brick that is added. Christ wants to be your cornerstone in your family, finances, dreams and plans. He does not want to restrict you but instead He wants to underpin you and help what you build stand. Where do you need to go back and check the cornerstone is present? We can all say we serve God, we love God but making Christ the cornerstone of our lives is a deliberate decision and changes the whole way we build.

As I write these words I am surrounded by the noise and activity of builders in my home and I can see where they have laid the cornerstone for an extension we are adding. Each day they lay more bricks and move materials around but not once has the cornerstone been touched. It is the permanent foundation in the changing structure; it is the reference point in all the other activity. We need in the busy of our lives to keep our awareness on the cornerstone so every other part of what we are seeking to build has a point from which it gets its true alignment.

BLESSING AND BURDEN

Finally, be strong in the Lord and in His mighty power. Put on the full armour of God, so that you can take your stand against the devil's schemes. For our struggle is not against flesh and blood, but against the rulers, against the authorities, against the powers of this dark world and against the spiritual forces of evil in the heavenly realms.

Ephesians 6:10-12

We need more awareness when we build of the blessing and the burden. Sometimes I get the impression that people live continually surprised or caught off guard by the things that are happening around them. From the betrayal they never saw coming to the burden they feel suddenly loaded down with. They can seem shocked and in those moments the lack of awareness can cause a loss of progress and even cause us to regress. Jesus lived fully aware of the blessing and the burden of ministry. He was fully aware of the blessing and burden of a team. He walked with those who would bless Him and betray Him. He needed to chose not just to be aware of the good but also the bad. He told his disciples in John 15 they would be hated and despised as He was. He told us in this life we would have trouble. Why give such bad news? Because your life needs the right amount of awareness so you can do the work of preparation.

I am one of those people who imagines the worst case scenario when it comes to starting a project or stepping out into something new. It's not that I don't have faith or I am filled with distrust but rather I have learnt it's my awareness that protects me. Despite their closeness, Jesus all the while knew Judas was going to betray Him. He lived aware, which meant that when the betrayal happened, though it hurt Jesus, it did not harm His ministry. Jesus knew Peter would deny him and yet He still loved him. His awareness was protection for what would otherwise have been like poison. The call to serve God involves a constant navigation of the blessing and the burden, the hard and the healing, the pain and the purpose. Live aware, like Job, that we need to be able to accept both the good and the not so good if we want to survive.

Immaturity needs everything to be good to see the good while wisdom knows that people are people and none are perfect, so to expect no loss or hurt is foolish. What is better is to prepare so when it happens, our heart can handle it. Gideon had an identity issue as he struggled to see his own abilities and to make matters worse, God took his army base down from the thousands to the hundreds. This elimination procedure was not to make Gideon's task harder but actually to make him stronger. If he needed all those people for him to feel he was able, then all it would need was one loss for him to feel he could go no further. It was God's way of showing Gideon right from the start where his help came from. It was moving his awareness away from the power of his troops into the awareness that his victory was in God's hands. It would be Gideon's awareness of that fact that would see him step into battles that in the natural he had no way of ever winning. He had an awareness that went beyond what he could see to what was unseen.

CHAPTER NINE

We need to live our lives more aware than ever that we have a real enemy but we also have the victory. We need to be more aware that the fight we are in is not against flesh and blood and therefore demands a different response from us. I used to have poor eyesight; I wore glasses and eventually moved onto contact lenses but when I didn't have my lenses in, my eyes would struggle to make out things in the distance. The hassle of the contact lenses helped me make the decision to get my eyes lasered. The idea of someone burning my eyeball didn't thrill me but the bigger gain of being able to see clearly was enough of an incentive to put up with the surgery. I will never forget the day after the surgery waking up and opening my eyes and I could see without the need for my glasses. It was so liberating, a whole new world of ease was at the other side of the pain of the previous day. Sometimes we spiritually need our eyes lasering, the scales removing. We have allowed our spiritual eyesight to weaken and the only way to see clearly is to pray bold prayers and allow God to show us things that our natural eye is struggling to discern. Maybe all you see is pain but God wants to show you purpose. Maybe all you see is how alone you are but God wants to show you that you are surrounded. For our lives to be beyond in awareness we need the ability to see beyond our circumstances.

The Bible tells us to dress up in the armour of God every day. Just as each day we get up and get dressed so we are appropriately clothed, we need to adopt the same discipline in our spiritual lives. If we live in ignorance to the hidden dangers of the enemy that prowls around our lives, this will cause us to become complacent about how we clothe ourselves spiritually. When we choose to be proactive about what we wear, we become less reactive in how we live. When you put on the armour of God first it helps guide you with every other item you may choose to add. When you put on the helmet of salvation, it guards your mind and helps you select what gets your attention. When you put on the belt of truth, it helps you know when you are being asked to watch a dog that is not yours to guard. When you carry a shield of faith, you can see beyond the circumstances and therefore choose not based on fear but faith. The breastplate of righteousness serves to make you aware of the choices you make and the people you involve. The idea isn't that we put armour on only when the fight seems to intensify but that we know how to live with our life covered and protected. God wants you aware not so you are scared but so that you can live prepared.

BEYOND
AWARE

THE CHALLENGE

SEE IT

Therefore put on the full armour of God, so that when the day of evil comes, you may be able to stand your ground, and after you have done everything, to stand. Ephesians 6:13-17

This month it's time to resign from some of the places where you have become the dog watcher. Identify the things you need to stop saying and doing and focus on the choices you need to start making that move you out of that place of compliance. This is only possible if we start to see how God wants us to clothe ourselves. We need to be able to visualise a whole new wardrobe that He has made available for us. You don't have to let the challenges of life dress you today, instead let's examine God's wardrobe and see if it's something we are already wearing or whether we may need to start dressing correctly.

_____

_____

_____

_____

_____

_____

_____

_____

_____

_____

_____

_____

_____

_____

_____

_____

_____

_____

_____

_____

_____

_____

_____

SAY IT

Let's look at each piece of armour and ask, how are we going to speak it out and act on it in each area of our life?

with the belt of truth buckled around your waist

Confess truth over your day; when you wake up don't allow a lie or wrong perspective to shape how you dress. The truth around your waist holds you together, it allows you to hear and see correctly, so read truth: open your Bible everyday this month and challenge yourself to be more aware of what God says than what others are saying.

with the breastplate of righteousness in place

Doing what's right is not coincidental or casual, it is a deliberate decision. When you dress daily with righteousness, you avoid compromise. This isn't being judgemental but rather it is making the decision to choose what's right over what's popular.

with your feet fitted with the readiness that come from the gospel of peace

Don't get dressed with stress this month, walk in the shoes of peace. Avoid the drama and if it asks for your opinion, let peace answer. Count to ten, or to 100 if you need to: give peace the chance to replace your need to act impulsively.

take up the shield of faith, with which you can extinguish all the flaming arrows of the evil one

Faith needs to be picked up and held up. Don't hide your faith this month, challenge yourself to have the faith that shields what you know is right. Shield what needs to be protected and pray and act in faith, not fear of what others may think.

take the helmet of salvation

Live aware this month of your salvation, of what you are saved from and what you can be victorious in. Don't allow defeat to write the wrong report. If you feel overburdened, then put on the helmet of salvation and walk in the power of what you are saved for.

the sword of the Spirit, which is the word of God

The word of God is your sword and the best way to fight is not with our words but God's words. Use this sword when you face a challenge - allow the Holy Spirit within you to guide your conversation.

DO IT

Make a plan of how you will daily dress in this armour. Make a check list of the items you find hardest to remember to pick up and put on. Just as you have your wardrobe essentials in the natural, have them in the spiritual. Make a commitment each day to dress correctly and as you do, note down the differences dressing well makes to your life and the things you are able to replace now that you have a whole new wardrobe.

CHAPTER TEN

BEYOND
COURAGE

BEYOND COURAGE

The Spirit of the Sovereign Lord is on me, because the Lord has anointed me to proclaim good news to the poor. He has sent me to bind up the brokenhearted, to proclaim freedom for the captives and release from darkness for the prisoners, to proclaim the year of the Lord's favour and the day of vengeance of our God, to comfort all who mourn, and provide for those who grieve in Zion—to bestow on them a crown of beauty instead of ashes, the oil of joy instead of mourning, and a garment of praise instead of a spirit of despair.

Isaiah 61:1-3

Remember that old classic film, The Wizard Of Oz? The story follows the journey of Dorothy and the companions she meets along the way: a tin man, a scarecrow and a cowardly lion. They are off on an adventure to ask the Wizard for the things they wish for the most: Dorothy wants to go home; the scarecrow wants a brain; the tin man wants a heart and the cowardly lion, well he wants courage. Along the way they face challenges and fight some very scary monkeys. The film ends as they are finally before the Wizard who informs them that what they had wished for all this time, they already had. The cowardly lion was not a coward after all, he was in fact courageous. He had already fought the evil witch and her army and protected a scared Dorothy. He was not as his name suggested, he had wrongly labelled his life. He was a courageous, bold lion. The courage he was searching for had been dormant within him all along. It was only awakened when he faced a fight he would never have thought he was qualified to win.

I think many times we are just like that lion. We have said I can't do it, we have allowed intimidating events or people to make us feel small, we have named ourselves cowardly when we are in fact stronger and more courageous than we realise. We are children of God and in Revelation 5:5, our Heavenly Father is described as a lion: "See, the Lion of the tribe of Judah, the Root of David, has triumphed". Scripture also tells us that "the righteous are as bold as a lion" in Proverbs 28.1. Therefore our true nature, which can only ever be found by looking at our Creator, is one that is courageous. The problem is we have defined courage through the world's eyes, where it has to be an heroic act or a moment that stands out in the crowd. This means we overlook the opportunity to be courageous in our everyday lives. We need to move beyond this restrictive narrative and take a journey that leads us to discover what was always within us.

You are made to have a courage that goes beyond, a courage with your words and actions, a courage to choose what's right in the face of what's wrong. A courage to silence the lies of an enemy and live free, a courage to dream big and believe for more. A courage to step into new waters and a courage to admit that you need a Saviour. A courage to try and a courage to try again when you fail. You are made to be courageous so what can you do to discover the beyond courage that's inside you?

CHAPTER TEN

Courage To Do Something

In 1 Samuel 25, there is a story recorded where David and his men were tired and sought some rest and food from a man named Nabal. David's men had protected Nabal's land for some time and so this request was not without merit. However, Nabal, whose name even means fool, was a very harsh man and he responded rudely, refusing to help David and insulting him for even asking. This put David in a furious rage and he ordered his men to go and attack Nabal and his household. When Abigail, Nabal's wife, was told of what was happening, her first response was, how can I help? She looked at her own small frame and her lack of authority; she thought she was not courageous. Her response seemed so foolish as she loaded a donkey with cakes to go and beg David not to harm her people. Yet Abigail's actions saved her entire household; she was indeed more courageous than she realised.

The courage was awakened because rather than ignoring the problem, she decided to do something to try and be a part of the answer. Abigail knew it was unjust for innocent people to lose their lives; it would be wrong for her to do nothing. Her plan was a demonstration of a beyond courage to defend those who were in danger. Beyond courage is not found in the grand gesture, it's found in the willingness to act on behalf of those who cannot. Her courage was in her commitment to not sit back and watch unnecessary bloodshed and that's exactly how we find our courage too.

God has made you and I to be those who defend the helpless, to speak up for those who have no voice. It says in Isaiah 61 that the Lord has anointed me: the anointing is attached to an action and comes on us when we move beyond accepting the status quo and realise we have a courage that can change it. It is when we allow God to lead us that He will place us into situations that will cause courage to find its voice.

Abigail's cake and donkey outing didn't look like it would make a difference but it was her courage to do something that God anointed. In the end it was this courageous beauty that caused David to not only cancel his plan to harm her household but also to fall in love with Abigail and when Nabal died, to make her his wife. Courage is attractive, it makes your life stand out. It isn't pushy or showy, it doesn't need to shout for attention. It can be like the quiet courage of Abigail or the unsure and insecure courage of Moses. His courage didn't come because he thought he was greater than Pharaoh but rather because he realised that His God was greater and would anoint His obedience.

COURAGE TO
SAY SOMETHING

"For if you remain silent at this time, relief and deliverance for the Jews will arise from another place, but you and your father's family will perish. And who knows but that you have come to your royal position for such a time as this?" Then Esther sent this reply to Mordecai: "Go, gather together all the Jews who are in Susa, and fast for me. Do not eat or drink for three days, night or day. I and my attendants will fast as you do. When this is done, I will go to the king, even though it is against the law. And if I perish, I perish."

Esther 4:14-16

We have all been in that awkward situation when a conversation takes a turn into an alley you would rather not be in. Maybe the tone of the conversation is negative or the purpose of the conversation has moved from information to gossip or perhaps it's that the subject being discussed is causing a dispeace within you. In those moments, we all have choices to stay quiet, to exit the conversation or to have the courage to speak up. I remember so many times at university finding myself in these kind of situations, when the opinions being expressed caused me to feel uncomfortable but knowing that if I said anything, that would potentially create a bigger challenge. I knew I had a voice and I had something to say but finding the courage to speak up is something we can all struggle to do. We don't have a problem talking, normal conversations aren't a challenge for most, but the times when our voice could make a difference are the times when fear tries to muzzle our mouths and intimidation tells us that we have nothing to say that's worth hearing.

Remember Esther who was happy to be a part of the harem in the palace, pampered everyday and living in beautiful surroundings? Yet she was brought into a conversation that was going to make her uncomfortable. Her uncle Mordecai got news to Esther that her people were in great danger. Her first response in Esther 4:11 was similar to the one we would probably choose: she didn't see how she could add in any way to that conversation. She wasn't a spokesperson, she was just an orphan girl in a place where you were not allowed to speak unless you were spoken to. Yet Mordecai was not just informing Esther, he was inviting her to enter the conversation. He was letting her know her voice was needed and that she was positioned in a place where her words would have more weight than anyone else's.

Esther just needed the courage to speak up. Her heart had to be moved for the plight of her people in order for her to find the courage to speak on behalf of those who had no voice. The more she thought about the cost of her silence, the more she found the courage to speak. Esther was an eloquent orator; she had no qualifications to speak to the king in this way but she was about to discover that the anointing comes on the words we speak that are courageous enough to challenge and change the conversation. You don't need courage to gossip, or courage to chat about things you are unwilling to challenge, but you need courage to speak change. You need courage to have words that bring correction, words that defend those who are defenceless, to start a conversation that is going to challenge the current choices and directions.

CHAPTER TEN

Esther knew when she spoke up it may be the last words she would ever speak. Her courageous words in Esther 4:16, "if I perish, I perish," became her starting point to move from behind the safety curtain of the harem. She placed herself in harm's way as she used her voice to approach the king and begin a dangerous and courageous conversation.

You too have courageous words inside of you and courageous conversations in front of you. What are you not saying, where or who are you trying to avoid? Perhaps those places and people need to hear your voice and you will be the one who is going to be anointed to speak up. Beyond courage has a voice and it is careful how it uses it. It knows words have the power of life and death and courageous conversations can change people's mindsets and choices. Esther spoke up and a whole generation was saved. Moses, who said he couldn't speak because of his stammer, was shown the plight of his people and this was his motivation to find his voice and to have the courage to approach Pharoah. When we choose to speak outside of our own needs and to give our voice to the needs of others, this is the place where we find we step into a covering and a sense of God's anointing that is the travelling companion of courage. An anointing that is attached to the outworking of our courage.

Where are you aware of words that need to be spoken? What if you were willing to be the one who said yes to finding the beyond courage to say something? There are so many places where the unwillingness to say what's true means more and more people are buying into the lie and accepting the deception as the reality. Just like in the fabel, The Emperor's New Clothes, lies are being passed off as truths. Someone needs to find the courage, like that little boy in the story, to say the emperor is naked, he isn't wearing invisible clothes, he is unclothed. We need our children to speak up, we need the church to speak up, we need an army of truth seekers to be courageous because it is often the ones who say something that can change everything.

Where do you see need, who can you help or serve, where can you be an answer? What cakes and donkeys do you have in your world? The everyday things you hold may seem insignificant but in the right setting are the exact things God will use to bring change and awaken the dormant boldness within you.

COURAGE
TO TRUST

___

At the first light of dawn, the king got up and hurried to the lions' den. When he came near the den, he called to Daniel in an anguished voice, "Daniel, servant of the living God, has your God, whom you serve continually, been able to rescue you from the lions?" Daniel answered, "May the king live forever! My God sent His angel, and he shut the mouths of the lions. They have not hurt me, because I was found innocent in His sight."

Daniel 6:19-22

We have all seen the demonstration in trust when someone is asked to fall backwards, trusting that colleagues or friends will catch them. The truth is, that isn't what courageous trust looks like. It isn't having the courage to fall into the known, it is finding the courage to leap into the unknown. If you have ever seen a baby about to try and take their first steps you will understand what courageous trust looks like. Of course the adults watching know that what the child is about to attempt is a natural part of their progression but to the child, this next decision to try and walk with nobody holding their hand is huge. They don't even know if it's possible but they are trusting the ones they love most as they call to them to let go of all they have known and take a step. Those first steps are pure trust, they have such limited understanding of what will happen next. They are trusting that what seems impossible will become natural. That baby has no idea of what walking will feel like and equally no idea of the freedom the decision to trust is about to bring them.

Though we are all past the stage of taking first steps in the natural, we are actually all faced with the opportunity to take more and more first steps in the spiritual and each set of those steps will require a new level of courage. Where you have already walked no longer requires you to trust as you know it is possible, you know that path but you need beyond courage to keep adding new first steps to your walk with God.

Daniel faced a moment when he was going to have to find the courage to trust way beyond what would be familiar or comfortable. His refusal to sacrifice his worship in order to fulfill the king's edict caused Daniel to have to make the choice between compliance and compromise or the potential loss of his life. Daniel chose to have the courage that trusted even though he had no idea how God would save him. He went into a lion's den not knowing if he would ever come out again but choosing to courageously trust beyond his own understanding. His trust had to go further than he had seen before. That's the kind of beyond courage we all have access to: the courage to trust God in a place that makes no sense and the courage that doesn't waiver in the face of such danger. The trust is not in what I can do but in what the God I worship has already said He will do. Daniel had a beyond courage to trust that the Lion of the tribe of Judah was able to triumph over the lions who were planning to have him for supper.

CHAPTER TEN

In order to trust with such courage, you have to have a faith that is louder than your fears. Courage that trusts in the most testing of times is only possible if you are brave but we have to trust in those first steps. The toddler trying to walk ultimately knows the one who is inviting them to take the step is the one who loves them, carried them, birthed them, so that awareness stills the nervousness and fires up the courage to step out. We have to look deeper into the face of the Father. We need to remember at moments when fear tries to sabotage our future the One who is calling us is the One who created us. If we are about to step into an unknown for the first time, we are trusting that we are doing it with the Almighty God who is all knowing and therefore we are able to be outrageously trusting.

Daniel's lions became his pillow for the night. What will courageous trust do for you? What obstacle will it make into a vehicle to move you forward? What barrier will it turn into a place of blessing? What challenge will courageous trust turn into an encounter that changes you forever? Be one who takes your courage beyond what you can handle into what requires so much trust it doesn't even make sense. Pray prayers that are beyond courageous, like Joshua who asked for the sun to stand still. His prayer in Joshua 10 was asking for something that was impossible but his trust was in the One he prayed to, the One who makes all things possible. Dream dangerous dreams that will not just change your life but will change the lives of thousands. Trust God with courageous faith in the face of crazy fears.

Beyond courage acts, speaks and trusts. It goes beyond what has been done before and creates new paths for people to walk along. Your courage is not restricted to one moment of heroism, it is a courage that goes beyond rescue into restoration and then beyond restoration into transformation and then beyond transformation into miraculous above and beyond provision. It takes courage to believe but beyond courage to act. It takes courage to see it but beyond courage to change it. God's anointing awaits our courage. It's His presence and power that accompanies our willingness to step into the problem and become the answer. So today, where is it time, like that cowardly lion, to awaken yourself? Where do you need to stop identifying with what you have been told or what others are doing? Where do you need to stop relying on others, when what you need is inside you waiting to be discovered? The righteous, that's you and I, are as bold as a lion. You are beyond brave, beyond courageous. So go ahead and roar.

BEYOND
COURAGE

THE CHALLENGE

SEE IT

When Gideon was asked to go in the strength he had, he first had to start to see things differently, he had to replace his image of being the weakest with an image of being more than capable. David had the same struggle, to stop seeing himself as the smallest, youngest shepherd boy and start seeing within himself a leader, a giant slayer. How we see ourselves will either feed courage or starve it. This month, examine what you see, where do you need to change how you view an area of weakness so that you can find boldness? Take a good look through your life, find where you have become caught up in things that are keeping you small. Be honest with yourself and name the areas where you need the courage to walk away, end the conversation or act differently.

SAY IT

Make a list of the places where you have lost your voice and you need the courage to start a new conversation. Maybe it's to challenge a behaviour or an attitude. Maybe someone or something needs your defence. The courageous conversation you need to enter might be about another's honour and future. We encounter so many people in our lives but it takes courage to start a conversation on purpose, one that may challenge or change the whole direction of the dialogue. So go ahead, write your own script and begin to change some of the lines you speak over your own life and the lives of other people. Where do you need to take back the control over the conversation that is out of control? Speak God's words into your areas of confusion and align the content of the conversations with the cornerstone of His word.

DO IT

When was the last time you made a decision that placed you on the edge and handed over your trust and faith in greater measure to God? Let's fill this month with courage: make a plan in a few areas of your world where you are going to step up with more boldness. Like Abigail, use what you already have to become more courageous. Then, at the end of the month, look back and see how far your courage has taken you and in what you new ways that courage has grown you.

NOTES

CHAPTER ELEVEN

BEYOND THANKFUL

BEYOND THANKFUL

Rejoice always, pray continually, give thanks in all circumstances; for this is God's will for you in Christ Jesus.

1 Thessalonians 5:16-18

As a family we have many traditions, as I am sure do you. One of my favourites has to be our annual Thanksgiving gatherings. As our family is half British and half American, we officially brought this holiday into our home and life. We have been on a campaign to spread it into as many other lives as possible because the truth is, we all need the reminder of the power of thanksgiving.

We can so easily forget all we have because we become so fixated on all we feel we still need. When we choose gratitude it disarms greed and makes us mindful of the goodness in today instead of obsessing about the desires for our future. Thankfulness acts as a prevention when it comes to feeling entitled and stops our hearts from becoming familiar with what we should alway hold as precious.

Our lives should be a living example of gratitude when we simply stop for a moment and consider all God has already done for us. That in itself should be enough to fill a thousand lifetimes with thanksgiving. Not one of us deserved the forgiveness He lavished on us, the kindness He has shown us, the grace and mercy that is daily extended to us. How often do we forget to say thank you for the gifts we are freely given and we could never afford to buy?

We all have areas where our gratitude could expand and our commitment to being thankful could go beyond the usual and start to set a different example. Have you ever given someone a gift and their response was, well let's say, underwhelming? Maybe you sent someone a present and they never even acknowledged they had received it. You were left wondering if the gift had arrived and then had to decide: should I ask them if it came as I have heard nothing or do I assume they got it but don't like it? Their lack of thankfulness leaves you questioning the quality of the gift. Though we should never allow our giving to become based on another's receiving, we should learn in the void of gratitude how much better it is to fill the atmosphere with thanks. Just as a lack of gratitude can create an atmosphere, an outpouring of gratitude can do the same.

CHAPTER ELEVEN

We can all remember when we did something for someone or gave a gift and the response from the recipient was above and beyond grateful. I have the privilege every year of blessing incredible individuals and families with gifts that make their lives easier, alleviating some of the pressure from their world in a practical way. Through the Cherish Foundation and Dare To Be, I watch families respond in some of the most breathtaking ways. The tears of joy, the gasps of disbelief at the kindness they are receiving, the relief as the gift is passed over and the screams of thanks and even silent, breathless hugs that say, I am beyond grateful. Those moments have marked my life in a way that outlives the gift giving and they have become a picture I hold in my heart of a way I want to live. Those moments become the encouragement to my soul to keep living in a way that is committed to giving. Thanksgiving is a source of food to every weary soul and a sign to keep living generously because your sacrifice isn't wasted.

A goal I have set for my own life is to keep that sense of overwhelming gratitude for the gifts I handle every day. The gift of my children, my marriage, the gift of friendship, the gift of someone's love and care. What if we could all become better at giving thanks? How would that not only impact the ones we are thankful for but also shape our own lives? How would that attitude of overwhelming gratitude change our conversations and guide our responses? What if living beyond thankful could move our lives into another level of peace and contentment? What if the antidote to envy and comparison was as simple as gratitude and thanksgiving?

We live in a world where our appreciation can be marred by the enemy called comparison. We are thankful until we see someone else did better, got something greater, was more successful or seemingly has more to be thankful for. We downgrade our gratitude based on a social media post or a Facebook feed. Comparison will steal your thanksgiving. We have allowed the world to dictate what success looks like and in doing so have undervalued and taken for granted what another would treasure and treat with great care and affection.

Remember when you were younger and you got a new bike or a new toy and you loved it until your friend got a better bike or a more high tech toy? In that moment of comparison you moved from grateful to jealous and that's how the enemy likes to work. If he can't steal it, he will try to downgrade it. If he can't kill off your faith he will try and stifle your thanks. If he can't destroy what you have he will settle for making you take for granted the things with which you have been entrusted.

What if we didn't let that happen? What if we decided not to be the ones who overlook the gift that each day is but instead decided to unwrap every day and see the beauty of what we have been given. To go beyond just feeling grateful by saying thank you and then to go beyond thanks by giving praise, giving expression to the thankfulness that the enemy would like to silence.

CHAPTER ELEVEN

"

WHEN WE CHOOSE GRATITUDE IT DISARMS GREED AND MAKES US MINDFUL OF THE GOODNESS IN TODAY INSTEAD OF OBSESSING ABOUT THE DESIRES FOR OUR TOMORROW

BEYOND PRAISE

As He was going into a village, ten men who had leprosy met Him. They stood at a distance and called out in a loud voice, "Jesus, Master, have pity on us!" When He saw them, He said, "Go, show yourselves to the priests." And as they went, they were cleansed. One of them, when he saw he was healed, came back, praising God in a loud voice. He threw himself at Jesus' feet and thanked Him— and he was a Samaritan.

Luke 17:12-16

Let me remind you of the story of the beyond thankful leper found in Luke 17. Ten lepers encountered Jesus, ten outcasts who came to ask Him to relieve their misery so they could rejoin society. Ten men who had no hope unless they were made well; ten lives that were marked by disease and doomed to die without a miracle. Jesus was about to give these ten men the one thing that would change everything. The miracle was not just the gift of healing but the gift of a new beginning and the gift of reunion with family and acceptance by their community. You would imagine that this beyond act of kindness and mercy would be met by an overwhelming and beyond act of gratitude and thanksgiving. Yet the Bible records that out of the ten who were healed, only one went back to say thank you.

I am sure the others were thankful and the excitement of the miracle was making them more aware of what was ahead rather than what had just happened. After years of pain and isolation though, was it really too much to ask to take a few moments to go and give thanks? The only one who returned to Jesus was a Samaritan, an outsider. This man was the most removed from Jesus and yet his thanks made him the one who came closest to God's Son. As the others were walking away from the Messiah, this Samaritan man was running towards Him with tears and shouts of thanksgiving. How often could it be said of those of us who know Jesus, who love and serve Him, that we can overlook the blessings that those who don't know Him receive with greater gratitude. Where have we allowed familiarity to take for granted what we should be at His feet giving thanks for? When do we allow our worship to be watered down because we are more aware of what we have to do next rather than the moment we have with Him? Where have we stopped praying with gratitude and instead come with shopping list prayers?

Beyond thanksgiving always comes back. This leper was on his way to the next place; he was like the others, about to go home and see the loved ones he had been separated from. When he saw the miracle he had been given though, he altered his plans and he went back. He didn't know if he would ever see Jesus again and he wanted to make sure he closed the conversation that began with a shout for help with a shout of thanksgiving. He went back and made sure that the ask was ended with a thank you. How often are we like these lepers? We have prayed and called out and as soon as we have an answer, we are on our way. We get so caught up in the excitement of the new possibility that we fail to remember the kindness of the One who made it possible.

CHAPTER ELEVEN

We can be so driven by the success, we can be so caught up with the new and the potential that we run from the point of breakthrough and forget our thank you.

Beyond thankfulness means we move past the pull of the adventure and always first come back to the place of surrender. I am sure like me you have prayed for favour or asked God to help open a door and when He has opened it you have been so excited and expectant. I have learnt in those moments the first thing that must happen, before I rush ahead, is to come back to that same place where I asked and now surrender the answer. Come back and say thank you and also ask, how do I use this now to serve You? If all we want are blessings then we will never bother to come back but if what we want is to deepen our relationship and register our gratitude, we will delay the adventure until we have come back and poured out our thanks, love and honour.

This leper came back and was shouting his gratitude. There was nothing polite about this thank you. It was passionate and it was over the top. This was a beyond thankful thank you. It was I imagine accompanied by tears and singing and wailing and praising. How often do we allow our prayer requests to be louder than our prayer response? How many times do we amplify our ask over our thanks? There is something powerful about giving thanks out loud. When we turn up the sound on the miracles and the answers we are receiving, that praise has power and that thanksgiving becomes other people's faith building. When you give your child or a friend a gift and they say thank you, that is always enough but when they shout it in action and in attitude, that becomes a beyond gift. That demonstration of gratitude propels you to keep going and keep giving. It's encouragement to the soul of the giver and now the one who was a blessing is being blessed.

Thankfulness is not only good for your own soul but it does good to those who hear it. We need to be louder in our gratitude than we are in our grumbling. Let our thanksgiving be heard more than our complaining. Don't be drowned out by the needs and instead turn the sound up on the ways God has answered. Let's praise Him loudly and in doing so let the enemy know our victory. Let's praise loudly so He gets the glory. When we don't give thanks then we can take far too much credit. Thankfulness is acknowledging those who made it possible and identifying that we didn't do this alone.

The Samaritan's praise moved his world from being a stranger to God to becoming the one who said, it's only because of God I can give thanks. He credited Jesus with his miracle and in so doing moved from being just one of the ten lepers to being the one who spoke with Jesus. Where do we need to turn the volume up on our praising and increase the amount of our thanksgiving? Don't be silent when it comes to your gratitude; go into that beyond realm and unleash the power that praise and thanksgiving can bring.

In Revelation 12:11 is says we overcome by two things: the blood of the Lamb - what Jesus did for us - and also by the power of our testimony - that's what we can do to glorify Him. Your gratitude is your testimony of what God has done and in that act of thanksgiving is the great power of overcoming.

"

TO EVERY ANSWERED PRAYER ATTACH YOUR MOST GRATEFUL RESPONSE. DON'T BE SO CAUGHT UP IN THE BREAKTHROUGH YOU FORGET YOUR THANK YOU

BEYOND
SURRENDER

Jesus said, "Were not ten healed? Where are the nine? Can none be found to come back and give glory to God except this outsider?" Then He said to him, "Get up. On your way. Your faith has healed and saved you."

Luke 17:17-19 (MSG)

When the leper arrived back to where Jesus was, he threw himself at His feet. This man who had only just been given the ability to walk out of his place of containment came back immediately and offered his life in service. This bowing at the feet of Jesus was an act of surrender and honour. The leper came back to bow his knee at the feet of the One who had restored him. In that moment, the Samaritan was bowing his agenda, he was surrendering his will and allowing his gratitude to guide his attitude.

When we are truly aware of all we have to be grateful for, it is overwhelming and will bring you to your knees before the majesty of the King of kings. The understanding that we have done nothing to deserve what cost Him everything causes us to live in humility rather than being haughty. When was the last time you found yourself at the feet of Jesus? When did you last take the time to just sit at His feet not for any other reason than to show how much you are grateful. When did you linger in His presence so you could lavish on Him your thanks? God will never demand this from your life just as you wouldn't from your own children. Yet this posture of gratitude draws you deeper. Stay long enough to surrender; sometimes it's a change in our posture that moves our lives to a place of beyond living.

The conclusion of this story leaves Jesus the healer wondering, where are the other nine, was only one grateful? I don't want my gratitude to be left in question. I don't want people around me wondering if I appreciate my life. I don't want someone else to be giving thanks for what I am taking for granted. I don't want my Saviour to wonder what means more to me, the answer to the prayer or the one to whom I prayed?

Jesus saw one man's gratitude had caused him to come back, led him to praise out loud and posture his life in an act of surrender. To that man He said, there is something your beyond gratitude gives you access to. There was a beyond miracle that his mindfulness created, which was the gift of wholeness. We see this same posture from the woman in Mark 14 who Jesus had forgiven, who came to wash His feet with her most expensive perfume before He went to the cross. She came to lavish thanksgiving on the feet of the One who had given her back her purpose and reason for living.

CHAPTER ELEVEN

She allowed her gratitude to change the entire aroma in the room that day, which made some uncomfortable; her generous thanks revealed the true heart of Judas. The aroma of her thanksgiving would go on to be the aroma Jesus would carry to the cross of Calvery.

Thanksgiving has within it the power of multiplication. Remember when the young boy brought his five loaves and two fishes to Jesus? He didn't have an answer for the five thousand plus hungry men that day but he knew he had something. He brought what he had and gave it to a beyond Jesus, who then did something that I believe was just as much a part of the miracle as what came next. He broke the bread and He gave thanks. He was grateful for the five loaves and two fish before it became enough to feed five thousand. His out loud thanksgiving for what He had been given became the breaking point of multiplication.

How often do we not give thanks because we wanted more, when actually the more may very well be locked within the thanksgiving we are limiting? When we live with beyond gratitude, we multiply miracles. When Jesus broke the bread, He didn't just feed the crowd but had baskets left over. When this leper came back to thank Jesus, he didn't just get the miracle of healing, his thanksgiving multiplied the miracle into his full restoration. His miracle looked different to that of the other nine who first came with their request. This man's willingness to go beyond prompted Jesus to also do something beyond. It's the child who is so grateful you want to bless again; it's the one who takes your kindness and passes it on that you want to entrust with more kindness. The beyond thankful heart takes the seed it receives and makes it become a harvest where others can feed.

So where can you become more grateful? Where do you need to go back, be at His feet or add volume to your thankfulness? Let's live in a way that is beyond thankful, not because we are hyping things up but because we have all too often played things down. Make a list of things you are grateful for and start to give thanks. Write down names of people you want to go and say thank you to, make a decision to live thankful and even if you feel you are grateful, go beyond, express even more. Even the breath with which you give thanks is borrowed. We are blessed beyond so let's give thanks beyond.

BEYOND
THANKFUL

THE CHALLENGE

SEE IT

Let's make this month a thanksgiving month. This is going to be fun. The first challenge is to take the time to see and make note of all the things you have to be thankful for. To make it easier why not split that into categories: thankful for friends and family; thankful for health and home; thankful for church and community; thankful for gifts and provision. Once you have your thankful list, your monthly challenge can begin. Everyday, take the time to think about and see just how good God has been to you in these areas. Choose one of the things on that list to focus on each day and actually take the time to express gratitude. Thank God for what you realise as you look again is such a blessing and commit not to take it for granted.

SAY IT

After taking time to give thanks everyday, then challenge yourself to add more thanksgiving moments. Show how grateful you are for the life you have and let that gratitude overflow into your attitude. If it's a person you are appreciative of, send them a note to let them know. If it's your health, do something to invest in that part of your world so you don't take it for granted. Lift your level of please and thank yous, speak out your thanks liberally. Be mindful of thanking those who serve you, from people in the coffee shop to friends who lend a hand, to the person who brings your post, to the teacher who helps your children. Speak thanks all month even if it feels awkward. Commit to a language of gratitude in the good and bad. Write, read, sing and speak thankfulness and journal how it affects your world and the world around you.

DO IT

Spend time this month growing in the understanding of the power of thanksgiving: study the goodness of Almighty God and declare your praise for all He has done. Thank Him in the good and the bad and be deliberate about taking the time, especially when it's hard to worship and bring a sacrifice of praise. Challenge yourself to be more expressive and vocal in thanksgiving to your Maker and watch how it will increase your joy in the everyday.

NOTES

CHAPTER TWELVE

BEYOND
BUDDY

BEYOND
BUDDY

A few days later, when Jesus again entered Capernaum, the people heard that He had come home. They gathered in such large numbers that there was no room left, not even outside the door, and He preached the word to them. Some men came, bringing to Him a paralysed man, carried by four of them. Since they could not get him to Jesus because of the crowd, they made an opening in the roof above Jesus by digging through it and then lowered the mat the man was lying on. When Jesus saw their faith, He said to the paralysed man, "Son, your sins are forgiven."

Mark 2:1-5

As we bring this journey of beyond to an end, I want to go back to our friend Buzz Lightyear. Remember at the start of all this, I wanted to make this book your Buzz Lightyear companion, the friend you didn't know you needed? Woody in Toy Story didn't see any need for a Buzz Lightyear in the toy box; he had his way of doing things and that had worked fine up to this point. Why introduce a new toy that would disturb the order? As all Toy Story fans know, Buzz was exactly what Woody needed. There was a whole world this friendship would open up to him; yes, that would mean at times things were more scary than safe but it would also mean more adventures would take place. Buzz's catch phrase, "to infinity and beyond", was an invitation to Woody to go beyond.

We all need those friends and as much as the words on these pages can encourage you to go deeper and explore further, it's easy to close the same pages and walk away and make no changes. That's why we all need some beyond buddy friends that we add to our life, not to make it more comfortable but to disturb the comfort. People we invite in so they can help us step beyond. These friends are different, in fact that's the challenge, sometimes it's the ways in which they are different that become the reasons why we never make the effort. Beyond friends may not be there all the time, they may even be friends that live in another nation but distance is not the issue because a beyond friend doesn't need to be in every place you are. That's not moving you beyond, that's simply adding to what you already have. They will suggest, stretch, expand your world through words, actions and invitations that say, let's go to infinity and beyond.

So how do you find beyond buddies? Where do they hang out? What social media platform are they on? Is there a beyond buddy matchmaking site we can download right now? We wish it was that straightforward but beyond buddies aren't bothered about advertising how great they are, they are too busy being great. So let's look at a few beyond buddies and maybe as we examine how they think and act you may realise not only do you already have some but maybe you also could become one for someone else.

CHAPTER TWELVE

Beyond Inconvenience

There was a man in the Bible whose story is not only about a miracle of healing but a testimony of what a difference beyond buddies can make in your life. His story is in the gospels of Mark and Luke. This crippled man could not make his way to Jesus; his physical state meant he couldn't walk, the crowd was so vast he had no way to get through. That man had lived with his disability for years and though the miracle maker was close, it just wasn't close enough for him to find his breakthrough. That was until his beyond friends showed up. They were not going to be deterred by the crowds, not put off by the inconvenience. They had a mindset that saw beyond all the obstacles, they only saw one thing, which was their friend needed a miracle and the Healer was in the neighbourhood. Every other detail on that day was unimportant to these four friends because they had already decided the outcome of the day: their friend who was lame would end this day well.

Beyond friends don't come over to sit and talk through your problem. They know what the problem is but all they are concerned with is getting you closer to your answer. Beyond friends are not put off by the inconvenience; they see this as an exercise to grow their perseverance. Beyond friends are different. These men came to the house that day with an attitude that changed the atmosphere. They entered with a spirit that said, let's go, we can do this. Their faith forged the way forward, not their fears or concerns. We all need these type of friends in our world. We need the ones who pull up a chair at the bedside but we even more need the ones who put you on a mat and get you to Jesus. These four men went beyond what was expected. They saw each problem as a provision, when he couldn't move they saw this as their opportunity to carry; when they couldn't get through they saw this as their opportunity to be inventive. When the roof was sealed they saw this as a possibility to make a new opening and when they saw Jesus was in the middle of His message they saw this as an opportunity to provide Him with a place to manifest a miracle. Jesus loves it when we find these kind of friends; Mark 2:5 tells us "He saw their faith". Jesus knew this man's miracle was because beyond friends had got involved.

Beyond friends help you become well. Beyond friends want you to walk and even better run. Beyond friends don't sit in the problem, they carry you to the promise. Where can you be someone's beyond friend? Where do you need a beyond friend in your life?

BEYOND INSECURITY

After David had finished talking with Saul, Jonathan became one in spirit with David, and he loved him as himself. From that day Saul kept David with him and did not let him return home to his family. And Jonathan made a covenant with David because he loved him as himself. Jonathan took off the robe he was wearing and gave it to David, along with his tunic, and even his sword, his bow and his belt.

1 Samuel 18: 1-4

We have all been in the scenario when we have had a friendship that was so good for so long but then something happened and the relationship changed. Maybe you got promoted and the dynamic in your friendship altered. Maybe you got a new friend which made the older friend insecure. Maybe you achieved something and the friend you thought would be pleased for you seemed upset or jealous rather than happy for you. Relationships can be complicated because people are complicated.

Back to our friends Woody and Buzz. The rivalry at first between these two characters for the boy Andy's affection almost destroyed the friendship before it had started. It takes a beyond secure friend to cheer you on into all that's ahead and that's why we need beyond buddies because without them, nothing changes. We don't grow, we don't think bigger or ask for greater. We are in fear of losing the loyal friend and so we never look for the beyond friend. God wants you to find both and they do exist: those friends who will cheer you further than they may even go. If you can't see any, there is nothing to stop you from beginning to become one for somebody.

Jonathan was a beyond buddy to David. Remember the story of when David took down Goliath in 1 Samuel 17? In that defining moment for David, two different friendships were offered. Saul wanted to befriend David as he saw in him something useful for his future but Jonathan also extended to David a friendship, not for what he could gain but for what he could give. Saul wanted to control David but Jonathan was a beyond buddy and even if David's success would mean he would not be the king's successor, Jonathan was secure. Imagine that kind of friendship, one where no title, badge or opportunity, no amount of blessing can spoil the purity of the friendship you have built. I have several beyond buddies in my life and they are hugely successful, brilliant and talented. It is my greatest joy to see them shine but that journey of becoming their cheerleader has been one I have had to learn from the hardest of lessons. I have been in friendships that I thought would last forever and found that the point of separation was where increase personally caused a friendship to decrease in its sustainability.

Sometimes we don't know where the breaking points are until the tide of blessing rolls in. We can be best of friends in the worst of times but what about best of friends in the most blessed of times? Those are beyond buddies, they are not threatened when your world increases, they aren't jealous over an opportunity you are given, they are

CHAPTER TWELVE

not possessive or restrictive. I remember not so long ago being in an interview with a close friend and though we were interviewed together, I was not asked one question directly. The friend I was with humbly answered the questions being asked by their seemingly super fan and I was so happy to sit and listen to the two interact. Not once did I feel, this is awkward or, what about me? As I was sat listening my friend turned the whole interview around to our friendship and began to share how hard it was when you are deemed as so successful to find those friends who are just ok with you being you. In that moment I remember thinking, being a beyond friend is one of the most beautiful things we can give each other. We release one another to be brilliant, never fearing that means we will ourselves be outshone. Isn't that the best way to live? I can't be you and you can't be me but I can cheer you on and you can cheer me on. Where are your beyond friends? The ones secure to be silent and secure to hold the door open as you step into new opportunities. Where are the beyond friends who say, I'm with you heart and soul and where can you become one for someone else? That dream you have will need a beyond friend to cheer you on so start sowing what you are asking God to reap in your own life.

Beyond Offense

Beyond friends are not going to quit when you offend them and you will, we all say things we wish we hadn't. We all have days when we mess up and cause upset. That means those closest to you may very well be offended and hurt by you but that's why you need to build beyond buddies into your life. They don't have an expectation on you that is unrealistic, they get it you are human but they are letting you know, my commitment is beyond the times I may be offended. Jesus was a beyond friend to every one of His disciples. He didn't just ask them to follow Him as leader but He himself committed to be their friend. He went beyond giving them a leadership training internship; He served and loved them and didn't leave them, even when they were failing or plotting to leave Him. His love for them went beyond Judas' betrayal, beyond Thomas' doubting, beyond Peter's denial. He loved them beyond the times they disappointed Him, disowned Him and deserted Him. In John 21 we are told that Jesus came back to Peter after the resurrection to ensure he knew His love went beyond the moment of failing. He walked with the disciples on the road to Emmaus in Luke 24.15 because He loved them beyond the confusion. He let Thomas put his fingers in His side in John 20:27 because His love wasn't offended by his doubting.

At times we have all drifted away from God or questioned His love for us and yet He has never taken offense and His love for us has never changed. A beyond buddy doesn't walk away when your words are harsh, they wait and they may even correct but they are going to love you beyond the offense. A beyond buddy doesn't try to win the fight, they don't care about being right, they care about the relationship more than they do the difference of opinion. None of this is an excuse to be rude or cause offense but it is a gift we can give those we love that lets them know, I am going to be the friend that stays beyond where others may leave.

This type of friendship becomes a firm foundation on which dreams can be built. It provides a bedrock of commitment that means you can scale new horizons. This type of buddy will always speak the truth but always do so in love. They become an armour bearer, a faithful fellow traveller. They will see it all and choose ahead of it all to remain with you through it all.

CHAPTER TWELVE

"

A BEYOND BUDDY DOESN'T WALK AWAY WHEN YOUR WORDS ARE HARSH, THEY WAIT AND MAY EVEN CORRECT BUT THEY ARE GOING TO LOVE YOU BEYOND THE OFFENSE

BEYOND BUDDY

BEYOND SENSE

Peter said to them: "You are well aware that it is against our law for a Jew to associate with or visit a Gentile. But God has shown me that I should not call anyone impure or unclean. So when I was sent for, I came without raising any objection. May I ask why you sent for me?" Cornelius answered…"Three days ago I was in my house praying at this hour, at three in the afternoon. Suddenly a man in shining clothes stood before me and said…'Send to Joppa for Simon who is called Peter…' So I sent for you immediately, and it was good of you to come. Now we are all here in the presence of God to listen to everything the Lord has commanded you to tell us."

Acts 10:28-33

Most of the ways beyond friends have entered my life have made no sense whatsoever. The coming together of our lives couldn't have been planned for or plotted out. In many ways it should never have happened and the more I consider how, the more I reach the conclusion beyond friends usually arrive simply through our acts of obedience. It's those moments when the Spirit prompts you to ask the question, reach out and help, show up or speak up. It's in those moments that make no sense that I have found beyond friends are formed. Maybe it will be geographically inconvenient, maybe it will mean an investment beyond what's comfortable, maybe it will be a stretch that makes you feel more exposed than you would like. Beyond buddies are rarely found in the familiar because they are there to take you beyond, into the unfamiliar. I have beyond friends all across the world; it means no sense that we would be greatest of friends but God doesn't need it to make sense for it to work.

In Acts 10, God told Peter to go and meet a man called Cornileus. This made no sense to Peter; this was going to the home of a Gentile and this was not the kind of friendship he was comfortable or familiar with. This friendship would mean that he would be with people who thought differently, ate differently and worshipped differently It didn't make sense but Cornelius was going to become the buddy that would move Peter's ministry to a place that would go far beyond.

What about Paul and Silas? A friendship that found them both in a prison cell in Acts 16. It makes no sense to have friends that get you thrown in prison for the sake of the gospel but God needed those men to have a relationship based on obedience not sense. That obedience saw them singing in a jail cell and making the most miraculous prison break together.

What about Shadrach, Meshach and Abednego? These three men found themselves victims of oppression, treated cruelly and thrown into a fire in Daniel 3. A friendship that would say yes to a furnace: furnace friends are hard to find. We all want to be friends with the one who has made it through the fire but to volunteer to be the friend that goes in the furnace with you, that is a beyond buddy. That friendship is not based on what feels or looks good but it is forged in the place of commitment to hold fast in even the hardest of times.

CHAPTER TWELVE

The list goes on and on of those friendships that don't make sense but without them destinies couldn't explode and beyond moments could never have happened. Ruth and Naomi had a friendship that made no sense generationally and promised no security, but that beyond friendship moved Ruth into the lineage of Jesus. All of these friendships that faced adversity and trial were united through one common factor, to put God first, to choose obedience over convenience.

One of the most treasured friendships I have came about from a moment that required obedience even though it made no sense. As I was worshipping in an event in the USA, I felt God tell me that the girl at the back of the room was to do with my destiny. Yep, that made no sense; I began to question was it even God until I was asked to introduce the guest for the evening. As I read out the bio of the girl I had never heard of before, the same girl at the back of the hall began to walk towards me. 15 years later, she is one of my most treasured beyond buddies. Our whole families now share and enjoy this adventure of life together. That one yes to God became a yes to each other and that yes changed my life and also changed the direction of my ministry.

Friendships like this don't need you to share the same street or even the same country, the only thing we need in common is our commitment to Jesus. Of course, I am thankful for the beyond buddies I have that live in the same time zone. I also know that if tomorrow that was to change, the friendship wouldn't, because beyond buddies don't change when circumstances do. They operate at a different level and with a different set of instructions. The attachment isn't based on the attention we give but on the intention by which we live. So don't ignore the moments when you may be about to bump into the friend you never knew you needed or even knew existed.

You may have too many friends like Job's in your world, voices that have talked you out of what God wants you to step into. Job's friends couldn't make any sense of the turmoil he was in but instead of holding their verdicts, they tried to make sense of what God was not wanting them to clarify. Job's journey didn't make sense, it was a testing that was nothing to do with any of his failings, in fact the testing was connected to Job's faithfulness.

In a time of severe loss, the only thing Job's friends could do was add sorrow; he needed a friend to encourage him, not make him feel he had failed. Job's friends tried to tidy up what couldn't be tidied up. God was going to go beyond in Job's life and repay him for his loss and more than that, abundantly bless him for what he had endured but in the gap before things become clear, Job's friends added more confusion than comfort.

The friends you have in your life are key. We can have many different levels of friendship and they all add something entirely different but we all need to ensure we deliberately add the friends that go beyond what makes sense. In those seasons that no one can explain to you and others may even avoid doing with you, beyond buddies won't go anywhere. They may not have any answers but their gift to your life is even when it makes no sense, they are steadfast.

CHAPTER TWELVE

"

EVERY WOODY NEEDS A BUZZ LIGHTYEAR - FIND THAT FRIEND WHO SAYS, "LET'S GO TO INFINITY AND BEYOND"

BEYOND
BUDDY

THE CHALLENGE

As you leave the pages of this book behind, my challenge to you is simple. Start to live beyond. If you're saying yes to going beyond, then I want to recommend you find yourself some Buzz Lightyear company. Maybe it will start with someone who doesn't even know you but you decide they can mentor you from a distance. Maybe you start to be the Buzz friend to someone else and by sowing you will reap that very same thing. Find those who say, let's go and those that when you do go, cheer you on all the way.

Go beyond in your ask, beyond in your peace, move beyond in your living and giving. Rest assured you still have miles to go before you would ever go beyond the God who has no limits, no end to His love and grace and mercy. There are oceans to discover, mountains to climb, adventures to be had. There are lives to rescue and pages to write, ministries to launch, families to raise. There are words to be spoken and songs to be sung, there are acts of kindness to be demonstrated and acts of justice to be administered. So what are you waiting for, friend? As Buzz would say to Woody, let's go to infinity and beyond. I don't know what that looks like for you but go for it. It's time to live beyond.

SEE IT

Write down the area where you need a beyond buddy and begin to see the type of friend that your journey may require. Then examine your own life for these qualities and while you are waiting for your new friend to arrive, think of ways you can improve as a friend yourself. Take the time to also write down the names of those who are and have been beyond buddies so far on your journey; see what strength they have added and examine new places that you can take that friendship.

SAY IT

Commit to going to someone in your world and saying you want to be their beyond buddy. Ask them how you can pray for them, where you can add strength to their life. Make a practical list of things you could do to help out this month - maybe it's babysitting or cooking a meal, maybe it's writing a verse out for them or connecting them with an opportunity. Take the time to make a plan of how you can say to someone, I'm going to be your beyond buddy.

DO IT

As you close the pages of this book, begin to think about your next chapter. Start making some decisions that a year from now will have moved you beyond. Take time to think back over the last 12 challenges: make a list of what may have been the hardest right through to the easiest and then write next to each area the steps you can take next year to move you even further beyond. Don't just be a hearer of the word, be a doer. Make a plan and start to take the steps. See your mountain, plan your course, start your ascent. Go friend: you got this and God's got you, "to infinity and beyond".

NOTES

NOTES

What miracle is within your very breath? This devotional invites you to go on a 365 day journey to inhale truth and exhale life as you learn to breathe again.

RESOURCES

Miracle In The Middle

Turnaround God

Identity

Be That Girl
Bible Study

We Are One
Bible Study

Outrageous Women
Bible Study

Teaching CDs

DVDs

Apparel

For a wider selection of Charlotte Gambill's resources, please visit:

CHARLOTTEGAMBILL.COM

CHARLOTTE GAMBILL

has an infectious love for life, a deep love for people and zealous love for God's House. Her passion is to build the local church across the earth, to see people reach their full potential and to develop and strengthen leadership. Charlotte is known for her practical, humorous and passionate application of God's word. Her messages of life and purpose are rallying a generation to embrace the broken and become ambassadors of hope.

Charlotte is an author, speaker, pastor and mother. She is founder and leader of Cherish conference and co-founder of Dare To Be, which reach thousands of women in the USA and Europe. She also leads Life Church alongside her husband Steve and together they have two children, Hope Cherish and Noah Brave.

Stay in touch with Charlotte on:

Twitter: @CharlGambill
Instagram: @charlgambill

Cherish Women's Conference UK

The Cherish women's conference unites women from all walks of life as one, to use their voice to glorify heaven and change earth. Cherish was founded more than a decade ago and now, every year thousands gather and lives are changed forever. We'd love you to join the party, just visit: *cherishconference.com*

 Life Church UK

Life Church is a vibrant, growing and multi-cultural church. We believe that the Church is the hope of the world and a place where everyone can thrive. One church in four locations: Bradford, Belfast and Leeds in the UK and Warsaw in Poland. For more information, visit: *lifechurchhome.com*

 Dare To Be Women's Ministry USA

When God put Charlotte's life together with her now best friend, Natalie Grant, they knew He was about to dare them to do something. Dare To Be was born out of simple obedience that has led to an incredible harvest. This annual event tours across America and invites women from all ages and stages of life to dare to be all God has purposed for them. To find out more about the Dare To Be tours, visit: *daretobe.com*

CG **Further Information**

For more information regarding Pastor Charlotte's ministry, itinerary, podcast, social media or any other enquiries, please visit: *charlottegambill.com*